YORKSHIRE MU

YORKSHIRE MURDERS

Paul Harrison

COUNTRYSIDE BOOKS
NEWBURY, BERKSHIRE

First Published 1992
© Paul Harrison 1992

COUNTRYSIDE BOOKS
3 Catherine Road
Newbury, Berkshire

ISBN 1 85306 196 4

Produced through MRM Associates Ltd, Reading
Typeset by Paragon Typesetters, Queensferry
Printed by J. W. Arrowsmith Ltd, Bristol

To my parents,
John and Mary Harrison

Acknowledgements

As a crime historian I spend many hours tucked away in the archives of Police Forces, libraries and old book shops searching for new and interesting information. Over the years I have spent literally thousands of hours poring over old documents and reports. It is an extremely interesting and satisfying pastime, if very time-consuming.

I am often asked how as a Policeman I can maintain an off duty interest in crime related subjects. Quite simply I enjoy it; the thrill of locating some obscure document which reveals part of England's criminal history can be enormous. The locating and collation of such information is just a small fraction of the work which goes into a book. The hours spent perspiring over a red hot typewriter formulating the material into a chronological sequence can be taxing work, and one often wonders if it is all worthwhile?

This is where team support is inspirational and it goes without saying that without my team I would have found it extremely difficult to complete this work. My sincere gratitude and true appreciation goes to Nick, Suzanne and Margaret of Countryside Books – there can be no better team in the business; to Lesley, Paula and Mark, my family, who endure my endless postulations upon case after case. My special thanks go to Sheila Wild, Librarian, West Yorkshire Police, John Goodchild, Principal Local Studies Officer and Archivist, Wakefield Libraries for his kind information, the staff of Leeds Public Library for all their efforts in locating obscure news clippings and to the kind people of Yorkshire who told me so many fascinating stories connected with the research into this work. My sincere apologies to anyone who I may have omitted from this list, but rest assured your assistance was appreciated.

Paul Harrison
1992

Contents

The Leeds Police in 1886 outside the new police station. Completing the line up on the left is a plain clothes policeman in his distinguishing bowler hat.

WITH MALICE
AFORETHOUGHT

MURDER has been part of our existence (or demise) since the beginning of time. It is documented in The Bible. 'Cain talked with Abel his brother: and it came to pass, when they were in a field, that Cain rose up against Abel his brother, and slew him.'

Heinous acts of murder have occurred throughout the ages with alarming frequency. Through common law, murder is defined as 'unlawfully, and with malice aforethought, causing the death of a human being, the death following within a year and a day'. It was through the commission of such acts that the principles of law and order were founded. The origins of policing in England can be traced back to the Danish and Anglo Saxon eras. The Saxons introduced into society a man called a tythingman, or borsholder or headborough. Ranking above him was the hundred man and the shire reeve (sheriff). These individuals were empowered to collect taxes and to enforce law and order. The term 'Constable' was introduced in 1252 and is believed to derive from the term 'Comes Stabuli' – Master of the Horse, an embodiment of both royal and communal authority. The officer held a high status amongst the community and was elected annually by the local community.

In 1285 came another milestone in the foundation of the English policing system. The introduction of the 'Statute of Winchester' gave further powers to the Constable and also introduced a system not dissimilar to town and rural policing systems. Watchmen were employed to assist the Constable in the execution of his duties, a watch, consisting of up to sixteen men were deployed at each gate of their town and these men were given the power to arrest offenders or strangers throughout the sleeping hours. Every man in such towns was more or less conscripted to this system and was required to work as a watchman. Failure to comply meant a spell in the stocks. Through time the office of Constable declined in importance until he had no more status than other members of the local parish, such as churchwarden. Later, the powers of a Constable which had always been at Common Law were gradually extended and by virtue of an Act of Parliament which stated:

'You shall swear that you shall keep the peace of our Lord the King well and lawfully according to your power, and shall arrest all those who shall make any contest, riot, debate, or affray, in breaking the said peace and shall bring them into the house of the sheriff. And if you shall be withstood by strength of misdoers, you shall raise upon them hue and cry shall follow them from street to street from ward to ward until they are arrested.'

In reality this power ordered the Constable to detain offenders and to keep them at his house until such times as they were brought to trial! Any expenses incurred were to be borne by the Constable, which was a somewhat unsatisfactory arrangement. The term 'Hue and Cry' was basically a system where the watchmen or Constable would pursue offenders through the street making as much commotion as was possible, ordering the citizens' assistance to apprehend the criminal! It was not until the 19th century that the Police Forces of England and Wales were formulated. The foundation of the Metropolitan Police in 1829 was the instigator of town and borough forces throughout the nation.

The Municipal Corporation Act of 1835 led to the formation of the Leeds Police Force. Its first Chief Constable was William Heywood who served in the position for one year. Within one week of its foundation some 18 Constables were sworn in and by June that year the middle management position of Sergeant had been created. The Leeds Police

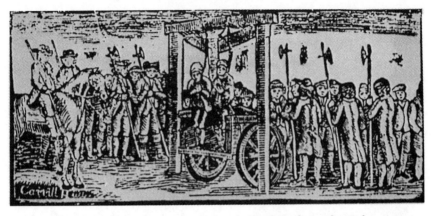

A wood carving depicting an execution at York in the early 18th century.

changed their title to Leeds City Police on the first day of March 1893 when by virtue of a royal charter Leeds became a city. Like Leeds, Bradford formed their own Police Force and became fully operational on the 1st January 1848 with William Leverett at the helm. Leverett had in fact been a Policeman in Liverpool prior to his appointment in Bradford on the 27th November 1847. Meanwhile borough forces were being created all over the county. They were regularly referred to by the media of the day as the town or city Police and it is interesting to note that with their inauguration there was more than one or two teething problems. The newly created Leeds force for example, were keen to display their adopted professionalism for the job, especially so as they were now being paid to carry out their responsibilities in a sensible manner. Unfortunately the force, known as the 'twenty men of Leeds' utilised the agents of the old system with similarly old ideas. The Chief Constable was a former Superintendent of the nightwatch and no less than four inspectors had been part of the old system, so things tended to stagnate for a while until the new style of policing forced a change in attitude. In York the inspector was not the paragon of virtue he was expected to be, for he ran a number of different brothels on a profitable arrangement and even introduced a system where crime complaints were investigated upon receipt of a payment which stood between four and five shillings!

The crime rate in Yorkshire compared to other counties was minimal. However, like all expanding areas it increased as the years progressed, the most disturbing fact being that murder was becoming more frequent. Though there was a high percentage of such crimes successfully solved there were still those which passed into the pages of the history books as unsolved and to this day remain mysteries of Yorkshire's dark past.

The mention of crime and Yorkshire to this crime historian always conjures images of vast moorland with the silhouetted forms of gallows standing proud on the summit of various hills. Such thoughts then turn to highwaymen and robbery and of course to the legendary Richard Turpin, whose real life antics were nothing like those which have been portrayed within the pages of various fictional accounts of his life. As Turpin was a murderer and was executed within the county I feel it only correct that he should be included in this compendium of murder in Yorkshire.

Richard Turpin was born in Hempstead, Essex on the 21st September 1705. His father, John, was a butcher and taught his son the basics of the trade. Turpin later spent some time in Whitechapel as an apprentice in the same trade, married and continued to work as a butcher. However, his interest in making money through more nefarious activities soon led him into a life of crime. Such activity did not go unnoticed and it was not long before a warrant for his arrest was issued. Turpin at once went into hiding, joining up with the then famous gang of housebreakers and thieves known as the 'Gregory Gang'. The gang's modus operandi was to identify a property which contained valuables. Then one member of the gang would knock upon the door of the property. When it was answered, the rest of the gang would rush in, restrain the occupants and clear the house of its goods. After a continuing number of crimes one by one they were arrested. It was during this period that Dick Turpin became

In 1737 Dick Turpin, England's most wanted man, added murder to his list of crimes when he shot a keeper of Epping Forest who was attempting to arrest him.

England's most wanted man, for he had added highway robbery to his list of crimes. Yet despite the authorities' various attempts to capture him, he remained elusive and so the legend began. Turpin was prepared to use any sort of violence in order to achieve his objective. A price of £100 was placed upon his head but this bounty was to double in future months as Turpin continued his crimes, increasingly involving violence. The south of England was in uproar as every inn and tavern was entered in search of the scoundrel, but Turpin was a crafty criminal. He had left these shores and it is believed that he visited Holland before returning in August 1736 and resuming his life of violence and crime.

On the 4th May 1737 Turpin committed murder by shooting a servant of one of the keepers of Epping Forest who was attempting to arrest him. Turpin was now a killer and the authorities were forced to make every effort to apprehend him. Again Turpin disappeared, gave himself a new identity and moved to another area.

'John Palmer' seemed like a reasonable sort of man to the landlord of the Ferry House Inn, Brough, South Yorkshire. He paid his bill on time and seemed to possess a generous personality. Approximately four months later Palmer moved to Welton and again gave the impression of being wealthy. In reality Palmer (alias Turpin) was continuing his life of crime. He had property in Long Sutton, Lincolnshire and used that address as a centre for his horse stealing operations. He retreated to Yorkshire when the going was getting a little too hot for him in Lincolnshire and people were becoming suspicious.

On October 3rd 1738 John Palmer was arrested for a senseless act. He had returned from a shooting expedition and in high spirits shot dead a cockerel in a street in Welton. A man called Hall was angered by this immature act and told Palmer how foolish he was. Palmer turned to Hall and told him that he would do the same to him if he did not go away! Hall at once reported the incident to the authorities and made a complaint about Palmer to a local Constable, and Palmer was duly arrested and brought before Mr Cowle the local magistrate at the Beverley Sessions. The magistrate asked Palmer to find sureties to support the fact that he would refrain from such nuisance behaviour, Palmer could find no one to support him. He was indeed a loner amidst the close community of Welton. Due to this fact he was committed to the Beverley House of Correction until such time that the matter could be fully investigated. Cowle was not happy with his findings and personally visited and questioned Palmer as to who he was and what he did for an occupation. Palmer explained that he hailed from Long Sutton where his father still lived but he had obtained bad debts and so moved. Further inquiries were made in Long Sutton where it was proved that Palmer had no relatives and that he was wanted on two counts of horse stealing!

Palmer was transferred to York Castle on the 16th of October 1738, charged with horse stealing. It seemed likely that no one would ever have considered that Palmer might be the notorious Dick Turpin, and had it not been for a quirk of fate they would not have. For whilst in detention at the castle, Palmer sent various letters to friends and family explaining his predicament. One letter was never delivered and somehow had found its way to Hempstead Post Office. In the Post Office at that precise time was a Mr Smith, an ex-schoolmaster of Richard Turpin, who at once recognised the handwriting as being that of his ex-pupil! With thoughts of a £200 reward he informed the authorities. The schoolmaster was taken to York Castle where a number of prisoners were presented to him, whereupon he identified Turpin without hesitation.

Richard Turpin was brought before the Honourable Sir William Chapple on the 22nd of March 1739 and was found guilty of two charges of horse theft and sentenced to death. On Saturday the 7th April of that same year, Turpin left his cell at York Castle and was taken by cart down Castlegate through Micklegate and onto Knavesmire. As the cart pulled beneath the gallows, Turpin, with the noose around his neck, ascended the ladder and voluntarily jumped off before the cart had drawn away, causing his own instantaneous death. So ended an era of terror for the affluent society of 18th century England. Sadly, much of the Turpin legend is mythical; for instance the famous ride to York from London. There is no evidence to support this claim, for indeed Turpin was known to stay at various taverns in Huntingdon and Cambridge in order to break the journey. The ride to York was first introduced by Harrison Ainsworth in 1833 in his fictional work titled *Rookwood*. Of one thing we can be certain, without the dogged investigations carried out by a Yorkshire magistrate known as Mr Cowle, Dick Turpin would never have been brought to justice!

As we progressed into the Victorian age the likes of Dick Turpin disappeared from our highways, the Police had improved their methods of detection and criminals now had to take more care in the commission of their crimes as any clues left at the scene could provide the detective department with vital evidence. Not all cases required the so called advanced thinking of a detective. For instance, a tragedy occurred at Fulstone, near Holmfirth in 1881 and required little in the way of investigation.

A local newspaper defined the circumstances excellently: 'Tuesday 6 December 1881; a distressing triple murder and suicide from Fulstone near Holmfirth. Henry Batty landlord of the Junction Inn, Fulstone, found that his daughter Hannah Moorhouse, age 27, was pregnant and already had three illegitimate children, Ada age 10, John age 6 and Emma age 2. Henry Batty was furious with his daughter and told her that she had to leave as he could no longer support her family, especially as another member was due. That afternoon he visited Huddersfield; his wife, son Henry and daughter and family remained behind. Upon his return he found that all the children were out which was nothing unusual to him. Some time later Henry junior returned with the news that Hannah had drowned herself and her children in the dam which was 100 yards from the house.'

Before doing so she had laid out linen on the side of the dam apparently to act as shrouds!

Although life was cheap in those difficult times no policeman attending such a tragedy could contain his personal emotions at the sight of a whole family being forced to such drastic actions. The death of innocent children is and always will be the most uncomfortable part of any policeman's task! The investigation skills necessary to close such a straightforward case as this would be fairly comprehensive, as the full reason for the murder and suicide would have to be defined as would Hannah Moorhouse's frame of mind, not something easily ascertained in Victorian society!

A case which could well have profited from the probing mind of a detective took place in 1832 before the founding of the new Police in Yorkshire. The Moorcock Inn then stood at the turnpike road running from Ashton under Lyne to Holmfirth and Huddersfield. The Inn was managed by the 85 year old William Bradbury, a man of an extremely miserable disposition. Also residing at the Inn was Thomas Bradbury, a 46 year old gamekeeper, who was not dissimilar to his father in terms of personality. In 1829 there had been strong suspicions that William Bradbury had been poisoning dogs who strayed onto his property. This caused much grief among local residents but there was little in the way of evidence to support their beliefs, and as a result of these incidents there was a great deal of animosity between Bradbury and some members of the community. By 1832 the alleged actions of William Bradbury had all but disappeared from everyone's thoughts as life in this secluded part of Yorkshire went on serenely. Early in the evening of the 2nd of April a traveller from Manchester was passing the Moorcock and was curious to see and hear activity from within. It was not the usual bar room joviality but something quite different. Perhaps he sensed danger, but whatever he conjectured, he continued along his way.

The following morning William Bradbury's granddaughter, Amelia Winterbottom, visited the Moorcock and was startled to find that the interior was almost completely wrecked! Peering about among the damaged furniture she saw blood upon the floor and at once ran to the home of a neighbour, Jim Whitehead. She explained her consternation at her awful discovery and Whitehead at once went to the Inn and must have been sickened by the sight which greeted him. Tom Bradbury lay upon the floor, plastered in blood which had gushed from the numerous wounds to his body and now surrounded him like a scarlet silhouette. Amazingly he was still alive, but only just, while close to his body lay a broken spade and a poker, which seemed to have been the weapons of attack. Searching for old Will Bradbury, Whitehead climbed the blood spattered stairs and located the old man in his bed. He too had suffered grave wounds from an attack, and his life too was hanging by a thread. Whitehead attended to the old man who was trying to speak

In 1829, innkeeper William Bradbury (on the left) and his son Thomas, were horribly murdered whilst alone in the Moorcock Inn.

and the word 'Pats' was whispered by Bradbury. Neither man survived their injuries and a murderer was now sought among this quiet country community.

It was ascertained that £7 in cash was missing from the Inn and thus the motive for the crime was invented. I say invented as the actions seem rather exaggerated for a simple theft. The key to the case ran much deeper than the obvious assumptions. An investigation into the word 'Pats' revealed that this was a term used by Bradbury in describing members of the Irish community. It was known that members of such a fraternity were working at Greenfield and it was soon confirmed that three Irishmen had been sighted on the road near to the Inn on the day in question! A man called 'Irish Jimmy' was arrested. He had blood on his shirt and seemed a likely suspect. However, he provided sufficient information to secure his freedom without any charges being brought.

The authorities seemed at a loss as to the identity of the killer and relied upon local information to point the finger of suspicion. On the 9th April James and Joseph Bradbury (who were no relation to the victims) were arrested at Huddersfield. It seems that Tom Bradbury was due to give evidence against the men for poaching offences on a nearby plantation and the case was due to be heard shortly after the murder. James Bradbury was heard to state that Tom Bradbury would not be giving evidence against them! Once again suitable alibis were produced and the Bradbury brothers were released and with them disappeared the last opportunity to solve the case. Despite spurious claims in recent times, the case was never solved.

Despite the increased efficiency of the policing system a number of murder cases remain unsolved within the county, including prostitute murders in Leeds, which to this day many local people still believe are connected with those committed in Whitechapel in 1888 by the notorious 'Jack the Ripper'. As policing progressed into the 20th century, Yorkshire was still tagged as the county of killers, a claim which has some reasoning behind it. The Acid Bath Murderer John George Haigh, spent most of his childhood and adolescent years in the Outwood/Wakefield area and subsequently Leeds. He is believed to have murdered eight people and disposed of their bodies in sulphuric acid in the 1940s. The Monster of Ten Rillington Place, John Reginald Halliday Christie, raised in Halifax, was responsible for the deaths of at least six women between 1939 and 1953. Even more recently we have Morley born and Bradford resident, Donald Nappey, better known as Donald Neilson, The Black Panther, who terrorised Northern England and murdered five persons between 1972 and 1975. With such horrors throughout the decades it hardly seems feasible that any other mass killers could exist within the beautiful boundaries of one of England's most picturesque counties, but further terror was to reveal itself in 1982, when one of Yorkshire's worst atrocities took place.

It commenced on the 17th of June 1982 when a young astute police officer carried out a routine traffic stop upon a green Citroen motor car. The officer approached the car and asked the sole occupant and driver of the vehicle a few courteous but pertinent questions. The officer entered the driver's name and date of birth into his pocket book before being fatally wounded by a gunshot wound to his head. The Citroen roared off into the countryside near Harrogate. The bravery, dedication and sheer professionalism of the wounded officer can never be truly epitomised; somehow, having sustained terrible injuries, he managed to scrawl into his pocket book the registration number of the car – KYF 326P – before expiring.

A murder hunt began, and the Police were fortunate indeed to possess more such fine officers. The pocket book entry revealed that the car was driven by a Clive Jones, date of birth 18th October 1944. Later that day the Citroen was found abandoned near Leeds. Forensic examination produced a number of fingerprints which when lifted and analysed were found to be those of Barry Peter Prudom.

Prudom fled Yorkshire and made his way to Lincolnshire where he broke into a bungalow belonging to an elderly lady. He took £5 from the house and tied the lady up, reassured by the fact that she would be found the following morning! The crazed killer then found his way to Girton, near Newark on Trent, Nottinghamshire, where he again entered a home but this time as well as taking food and money, he shot dead one man and seriously wounded his wife. Prudom then stole their Rover motor car. He made his way back to Yorkshire, Malton to be precise. The Police were on the lookout for England's most wanted man and had received accurate descriptions of him. At Old Malton Post Office two officers spotted a stranger who had purchased some food. The officers approached him and suddenly Prudom produced a Beretta firearm. Both unarmed officers ran in separate directions, Prudom followed one and finally caught up with him and as he attempted to jump over a wall, Prudom repeatedly fired, shooting the officer dead!

The killer then went to ground in the woodland close to Malton. His hideaway was quickly located but there was no sign of the man they wanted. On the 3rd July Prudom entered another home and held its three occupants as prisoners. He discussed his crimes and actions with the family and seemed to be attempting to justify himself to them. He left the family in the early hours of Sunday 4th July 1982. Prudom secreted himself into a hide he had prepared outside the family's home. It consisted of wood placed against a wall. The authorities had already located Prudom's whereabouts and waited for the gunman to make his next move. Prudom had resigned himself to a final shootout with the Police and despite official requests to confirm his identity and to leave the hide, he refused. Two stun grenades were thrown towards the hide and the shooting commenced, resulting in Barry Prudom's death, by virtue of a bullet fired from his own gun. (A number of other firearm wounds were evident upon his body thus proving the accuracy of the Police marksmen.) The 17 days of hell during Prudom's reign of terror are never to be forgotten by the people of North Yorkshire. As if the torture Barry Prudom forced upon the county was not sufficient, another more vicious killer emerged into an unsuspecting Yorkshire.

The crimes of Peter Sutcliffe, the Yorkshire Ripper, are well documented and I do not feel that there is any need to repeat them here, other than to add that once again that the killer had his roots in the county.

Yorkshire is one of the most pleasant counties in Britain. Indeed, having once resided in the county for several years, I hold fond memories of the friendly open attitude its inhabitants possess.

This work is in no way intended to be a comprehensive account of all murders within the county, but rather a small selection of those which I have found intriguing. Similarly I do not proffer myself as an exclusive authority upon those contained therein; like everyone else I strive to achieve as much accuracy as is possible. I hope you enjoy this brief visit into Yorkshire's murderous history.

Paul Harrison
1992

THE WICKED STEPFATHER

THE village of Great Broughton is situated close to the northern border of North Yorkshire. It is not an area where one would expect to find a multiple murderer, yet in 1753 three persons died as a result of the actions of one individual whose avarice was responsible for the deaths of two innocent parties as well as his intended victim.

William Smith was a well respected farmer residing in Great Broughton. He lived on the farm with his mother, who had recently married her second husband, one Thomas Harper of nearby Ingleby Manor. Harper already had two children, William and Anne, from a previous relationship. William Smith, like most sons, had been extremely close to his father who had taught him how to work the land for profit and utilise its resources to best effect. The sudden death of his father had caused Smith to grieve for many months and it is doubtful if anyone could ever fill the great void which now existed in his life. Most certainly Thomas Harper did not seem a suitable replacement. William found himself loathing his mother for attempting to replace his father with Harper. He felt that an outsider had no right to come into his home and dictate how the farm would be managed. Furthermore, not only had this outsider taken over the responsibility of running the farm but he was now interfering with the estate, a fact which caused William Smith great grief. Why should this man be allowed to walk into such wealth and determine how it should be spent!

The stage was set for domestic disharmony, arguments

were frequent and a great rift between natural mother and son began to expand. Smith could no longer command his mother's attention, nor could he persuade her to make any decision pertaining to the land and the farm. Everything had to go through Harper! Not surprisingly Smith's dislike of his stepfather ran deep, so deep in fact that it became absolute hatred. Such feelings caused Smith's mind to consider methods of eradicating the problem from his life. Death seemed the most effective solution; after all the farm and estate were by rights his, not Harper's! Over the weeks which followed Smith planned numerous scenarios based upon murdering Thomas Harper. Shooting seemed too obvious and the crime would be all too easily traced back to him. 'Accidental death' was perhaps the best ploy, yet the organisation of such an accident would be too time consuming and there was always the possibility that it would result in failure. Smith disliked confrontation and therefore murder by physical contact was out of the question.

There remained but one option, an option that so many cowardly killers have utilised, poison! No personal contact was required to administer such potions and it would seem as though he had not actually done anything!

William Smith visited a local apothecary and purchased some physic (a purgative drug) for his sick horses and whilst there he discussed with the apothecary the problem he was having with vermin infesting his barn. He asked what was the best way of ridding the farm of these pests. 'Poison' was the reply. Arsenic was a killer used by many to rid their property of vermin. William Smith purchased twopenny worth of arsenic and so the plan to murder had now gone one step further. On returning to the farm Smith found himself unable to put his plan into action. So the situation worsened as Smith became a virtual loner in his own home. His stepfather had long since given up any attempt to find favour with Smith and Smith continued to be obsessed with the thought of inheriting his father's estate and all the good fortune that accompanied it.

Good Friday 1753 saw Thomas Harper invite some neighbours to their home for some entertainment. William Smith entered the kitchen of the farmhouse and saw the maid making a cake mix. Without further ado Smith went to collect the arsenic from where he had hidden it and returned to the kitchen. The ideal opportunity for premeditated murder had presented itself to him for the maid was absent from the kitchen and the cake mix sat invitingly upon the table. Quickly, Smith walked up to the mixing bowl and poured in the contents of the bottle marked 'POISON' which he clutched in his hand. He then gave the mixture a quick stir in order that the powder should become inconspicuous in the mixture. Unbeknown to Smith, the maid had returned to the kitchen and was standing behind him. She did not, however, see him administer the poison to the mix and being only a servant she could hardly question him why he was standing so close to the baking mixture. So nothing was said and the cake was prepared, baked and served to the waiting family and guests.

Smith disappeared from the farmhouse area and into the surrounding fields for a few hours. When he returned the guests had left and life seemed quite normal. Smith became concerned about the poison and the cake mixture and on again visiting the kitchen, he saw that some of it had been consumed. Therefore surely someone had to die in the near future! Smith did not have too long to wait before he saw the wicked results of his actions. His stepbrother and sister, William and Anne Harper, became violently ill with severe pains in their stomachs causing them to convulse in agony, their screams of pain echoing throughout the farmhouse. Thomas Harper began to suffer from similar agonies and medical assistance was sought. With the amount of poison administered and consumed by the three there was little any doctor of that era could achieve. Their excrutiating agonies continued throughout the evening and the three members of the Harper family had no relief from their pain until the following day when all three died! It was obvious to those who saw the suffering of the Harpers that they had died as a result of poisoning. The medical explanation supported this fact; it was a case of murder! This was announced to William Smith and his mother by the authorities at the scene and such a warning was sufficient for William to depart the region. Panicking he fled to Liverpool where he remained for a few days. Correctly, the authorities assumed that such actions were those of a guilty man. There was also other evidence which more or less positively identified him as having both the means and the motive.

Within days William Smith suffered greatly from guilt. He realised that his arrest and detention was imminent, but he was prepared to face it in order that his father's good name could be maintained. As he had little in the way of funds to remain in Liverpool he was forced to return home in any case.

Smith was arrested and taken to York where he was brought before Mr Sergeant Eyre, at the Summer Assizes. The evidence of the maid from the farmhouse who had seen Smith standing over the cake mixture seemed to seal his fate. The apothecary told of Smith's purchase of twopenny worth of arsenic. However, none of these testimonies were necessary to prove the case, as Smith confessed to his guilt and was hanged at York on the 14th August 1753.

THE TOWTON TRAGEDY

THE introduction of forensic evidence into the English judicial system was a giant step for investigative authorities in their bid to bring offenders to justice. This case in question is quite remarkable for had it not been for introduction of such evidence, a killer would have escaped scot-free.

Towton is situated close to the centre of Yorkshire. Indeed, a tree in the nearby village of Barkston is reputed to be the very centre of the county. It is synonymous with the famous battle of Towton which took place on Palm Sunday 1461 in Towton Field during the Wars of the Roses. It is believed that upwards of 30,000 men died in the snow that day and many of these lie in the churchyard at Saxton.

Our story took place 472 years after the battle of Towton, but had similar results; death! Frederick Ellison Morton and his wife Dorothy Louise Morton were quite affluent, Frederick being the managing director of Cattle Factors Limited and a hard working man. His wife, however, was somewhat flighty. In 1930 she was caught in a passionate embrace with a man friend by one of her household staff, Ernest Brown. Now Ernest Brown had an evil streak within his personality. Armed with the secret knowledge of this illicit embrace he hounded Dorothy Morton and threatened to tell her devoted husband of her infidelity. Thus he was able to coerce her to have sexual relations with him on a frequent basis. These encounters were despised by Dorothy yet she had not the courage to confide in her husband about her blackmail or confess to her indiscretions. So the situation deteriorated. Ernest Brown persuaded himself that the

Freddy Morton, managing director of Cattle Factors Ltd, and devoted husband, fatally unaware that his wife was the victim of sexual blackmail.

sexual encounters were of a sincere nature, his mind long since blanking out thoughts of Dorothy's fear or oppression. In 1933 the Morton household moved from their Halifax home to Saxton Grange close to the village of Towton and Brown went with them as groom. He was given a hut on the premises in which he could comfortably reside.

After the removal it seems that Brown had in some way antagonised Frederick Morton, whose attitude towards him altered dramatically. Certainly there is no reason for believing that he was aware of the sexual relations between his wife and the groom, but perhaps he may have noted something odd about the groom in his attitude towards the lady of the house. In June of the same year the master of the house ordered Brown to mow the lawn. The groom was furious as he felt such actions were beneath his position and he point blank refused to do so and duly resigned from his position. Dorothy Morton realised that Brown would not simply depart without further efforts at blackmail and she was correct. For two days later he contacted her and demanded that she insist he be re-employed at the Grange.

She acceded to this demand and Frederick found Brown a position as odd-job man which angered him all the more, and such was the situation at the Grange during that summer.

Early in the morning of Tuesday 5th September 1933, Frederick Morton announced that he was taking his Chrysler car and going to Oldham with reference to a business matter. He expected to return later that evening. Dorothy Morton carried out yet another clandestine meeting, this time with another man friend with whom she went swimming at Wetherby. Ernest Brown was also absent from the Grange for most of the day for he had taken a cow to Greetland. During the journey he called into the Malt Shovel at Tadcaster to collect the landlord, Mr Wright, and together the men met with Anne Littlewood, landlady of the Junction Inn with whom Brown was having an unsatisfactory affair. The trio were out for the better part of the day and at 8.00 pm Brown left them at Tadcaster with the promise to Anne that he would return to take her to Leeds. He failed to make this meeting.

On returning to the Grange at 8.30 pm Brown saw Dorothy Morton and asked where she had been. The lady of the house told him the truth which angered him causing him to physically drag her out of the house! Thankfully Dorothy Morton screamed and was rescued by Ann Houseman, a

Saxton Grange, scene of the murder in 1933.

nanny at the Grange. Within a few minutes Brown then attempted to coax Dorothy out of the house. This time she refused claiming that she expected a telephone call. Brown was furious and stormed out into the yard. Dorothy Morton and Ann Houseman sat in the kitchen, both concerned by Brown's volatile disposition which seemed to be at fever pitch. Suddenly at 9.00 pm the silence was shattered by the loud report of a shotgun, the noise of which came from within the farmyard area. Moments later a second shot echoed around the yard and this time pellets rattled against the kitchen window panes. It was almost an hour before Ernest Brown entered the kitchen and explained to the worried women that he had spotted a rat near to the barn and had shot it. He returned the shotgun to the kitchen cupboard and seemed very complacent about something. About five minutes later at 10.05 pm the telephone rang. It was a gentleman requesting to speak with Frederick. He was advised to call back in ten to fifteen minutes which he agreed to do. Both women returned to the kitchen to see Brown taking a white handled game knife out of a kitchen drawer but neither dared question him as to his purpose for removing it.

It was now close to midnight and the two women retired to their rooms. But soon they realised that they would be safer together. Ann Houseman looked out of the bedroom window and saw Brown walk across the yard and enter the house by the back door. For a while there was much noise from the kitchen area but at around 2.00 am it ceased. The women were obviously worried as to where Frederick Morton was, but neither dare give voice to their feelings. Attempting to get a few hours sleep, the women sat together upon the bed, but their tranquillity was destroyed by a huge explosion and the room was lit up with a bright yellow and orange flash. Peering out of the window both women saw flames leaping out of the garage and high into the night sky. Explosion seemed to follow explosion as numerous cans of petrol ignited. Terrified, the women rushed downstairs but when they attempted to call for help, the telephone was dead!

Ann Houseman fetched the Morton's sleeping baby and the group then fled the house and hid in a nearby hedge until they were sure that Ernest Brown was no longer around. The odd-job man was running around the farm attempting to round up the terrified animals which were stampeding all over the place. Realising that such attempts were fruitless he took a horse box and drove it to the nearby home of Murray Stewart, a farm bailiff, unaware that Dorothy Morton, her baby and Ann Houseman were also heading to the Stewart home. The bailiff and Brown returned to the Grange and saw that the flames had now gathered momentum and set alight the other outbuildings. Hurriedly, Stewart returned to his home and rang the fire brigade and the local Constable, P.C. Broadhead, before he returned to the inferno. Fire tenders from Selby and York soon arrived on the scene and extinguished the blaze which had caused much damage. Constable Broadhead arrived accompanied by Dorothy Morton. She was shocked to see that her husband's Chrysler motor car was in the burnt out garage!

The burnt out cars in the barn, with that on the left containing the body of Freddy Morton.

Constable Broadhead approached the vehicle with some trepidation. Peering into the smouldering interior he saw the blackened and twisted form which at one time must have been a human being. The smell was overpowering but Broadhead was a good officer who knew he had a job to perform. Professionally he assessed the scene; beneath the car (directly below the burnt form in the driver's seat) he saw a diamond ring and two key rings. These were identified as the property of Frederick Morton. The ring had fallen from his burnt fingers onto the wooden car floor, which in turn had been destroyed within the blaze. Elsewhere Broadhead noted that the drainage nut was missing from the petrol tank. It seemed improbable that this could have fallen out of its own accord for there would be a necessity for pliers to extract the nut. Within a few feet of the wreckage Constable Broadhead found a pair of pliers and an adjustable spanner! This evidence was seized for future reference as the officer decided that this was more than just an ordinary accident.

Superintendent Dance and his colleague Superintendent Blacker were summoned to the scene as various witnesses would need to be interviewed by the senior officials. Ernest Brown was taken to Sherburn in Elmet Police station. At that point he was not under arrest but simply answering a few Police enquiries. With the chief suspect's whereabouts known, the Police investigation machine clicked into gear. General Post Office telephone engineers were called to the house in order to ascertain why the telephones were not working. It did not take them long to confirm that the wires appeared to have been deliberately cut. A post mortem performed by Doctor Sutherland confirmed that the body within the car had been dead before the fire began as no smoke inhalation had taken place, and in the lower part of the abdomen there existed a gaping hole. This was confirmed as a gunshot wound. To support this evidence several pellets were found in the heart. Frederick Morton had been murdered!

Upon hearing this news, Superintendent Blacker visited

Sherburn Police station and immediately cautioned Ernest Brown. He asked if the clothing he was now wearing was that which he had worn during the previous evening. Brown confirmed this fact and was ordered to undress. He was then provided with replacement clothing and held by the Police for further questioning. The clothing was taken directly to London where top analyst Dr Roche Lynch could examine it. Ernest Brown was then charged with the wilful murder of Frederick Ellison Morton.

An inquest into the death of Frederick Morton took place in the offices of Saxton Grange just three days after the dreadful crime. Ernest Brown denied all allegations put before him. Mrs Morton was called to give evidence and explained that the last time she had seen her husband had been around 1.30 pm Tuesday 5th September 1933. Constable Broadhead then explained the incidents leading up to him finding the body in the car. Superintendent Blacker then requested that the coroner adjourn the inquest for a month in order that all available evidence could be gathered and his request was granted.

The superintendent was efficient. He organised a search of the farm yard area in pursuit of evidence to support Brown's claim of shooting rats near the barn. No vermin nor any shotgun pellets were found which could have supported this testimony. The murder weapon and a cartridge were located and passed to Robert Churchill, a revered gun expert, for his analysis. The white handled game knife removed from the kitchen drawer by Brown was submitted to Professor Tryhorn, Professor of Chemistry at Hull University College, as too were the end pieces of the cut telephone wires. The professor took photographs of the knife blade edge and of the cut telephone wire. These were magnified up to one hundred times in order that discrepancies in the blade could be matched with identical grooves in the wire casing. They matched. In order to prove this the Professor again cut the wire using the knife concerned, again the results matched the original cut. The knife concerned had been the one used to

cut the telephone wires at Saxton Grange. The evidence
against Brown was now overwhelming. Despite this fact
Brown was not brought before Sherburn Police Court until
October 16th. Dorothy Morton was called to give evidence
and during a sensational two hour spell she outlined the
forced relationship with Ernest Brown and the threats he had
made against her. Doctor Roche Lynch, the Home Office
Analyst, told how he had found blood smeared behind the
toecap of one of Brown's boots. Robert Churchill, the gun
expert, confirmed that the cartridge found at the scene had
been fired from the left barrel of the shotgun found in the
kitchen cupboard and used by Brown on the night of the
murder. The defence made no objections to this evidence and
did not call any other witnesses, and so Brown was
committed for trial at the Leeds Assizes on Monday 11th
December 1933.

The trial commenced at 10.30am before Mr Justice
Humphreys, representing the prosecution was Mr Paley-
Scott KC and for the defence Mr Streatfield. The courtroom
was filled to capacity with friends of the Mortons and the
curious whose interest had been fed and instigated by the
press coverage of events. The jury were warned about
allowing press opinions to formulate their own opinions as
to the facts of the case and so the trial began. Brown pleaded
'Not Guilty' and so the witnesses were called. Dorothy
Morton seemed rather nervous about her version of events
which she had repeated on numerous occasions in previous
hearings. Gently Mr Scott led her through events as they
occurred, coaxing the truth from her. Mr Streatfield was
careful in his cross examination, his questions obviously
cleverly formulated. His initial question visibly rocked
Dorothy Morton yet it was an obvious query. 'Why did you
not inform your husband about Brown?' Dorothy Morton
contemplated for a few seconds as though to allow herself
time to compose herself. Suddenly she snapped back in a
very matter of fact tone: 'Because I was frightened to!' It
seemed quite clear that it would have taken an awful lot of

courage for her to confess to unfaithfulness, despite the fact that it was forced upon her by a vindictive man. One by one the witnesses gave evidence. The pliers found close to the burnt out car were introduced to the hearing and were identified as those belonging to Ernest Brown. Eventually after four days the jury were given the opportunity to retire to decide upon a verdict, but not before the judge had again advised them to think very carefully about the evidence. He stated that Mrs Morton by her own admission was an immoral woman, but because she was did not mean that she could not be believed. Closing, he claimed that due to the amount of unanswered data it was his feeling that the case for the prosecution could not be regarded by them as being complete.

The jury took a little over an hour to decide that Ernest Brown was guilty of murder. Perhaps it was one of the exhibits displayed in court which forced them to this opinion, as part of the dead man's skin displaying the gunshot wound was shown to them. Perhaps this was a deciding factor in this case.

The public petitioned for a reprieve for Brown but it was not forthcoming and he was executed at Armley gaol, Leeds on 6th February 1934. One curious point has since been brought to the fore. There are those who claim that Brown was in fact a double killer, for in 1931 a young girl was found badly burnt by her car close to Otterburn in Northumbria. The case was known as the Otterburn Murder. On the gallows Ernest Brown was approached by an official and asked if he wished to confess to the Saxton Grange murder. It is claimed that he murmured either 'Ought to burn' or 'Otterburn'!

THE MYSTERIOUS DISAPPEARANCE OF DANIEL CLARK

W HEN Daniel Clark left his Knaresborough home on the night of 7th February 1745 en route to a slightly suspicious business encounter, he could never have envisaged the ghastly consequences which were about to befall him, for this was to be the last night of Clark's life! His killers were not to be brought to justice for over a decade and the identity of the perpetrators of the crime caused it to become one of Britain's classic cases.

Eugene Aram was born in the charming village of Ramsgill, Yorkshire in 1704 and was of a good family. Indeed, one of his ancestors served as High Sheriff of the county during the reign of Edward III. Yet time had taken its toll upon the family wealth over the years and Aram was born into a financially impoverished environment. His father was a hard working gardener at Newby Hall, Ripon.

The young Eugene often visited Newby Hall to assist his father in gardening chores. During such visits the owner of Newby Hall, Sir Edward Blackett, would allow Eugene to read the books within the hall's generous library. This freedom allowed the youngster to profit greatly from the self taught knowledge gleaned from the volumes within the Blackett collection. Sadly, Sir Edward died and Eugene no longer had the opportunity to pursue his literary research. The Blackett family were loyal employers and in 1720 Christopher Blackett, (the son of Sir Edward) took young

Aram with him to London and employed him as a book-keeper, a position which suited him and in which he served very well. For almost 18 months Eugene Aram remained in London, visiting his family in Yorkshire as and when the opportunity arose. He seemed quite content with his lot, but fate was to play a cruel hand, restricting Aram's career and consequently changing the future outcome of his life. Aram was struck down by small-pox. He became so ill that he was forced to return to the family home in Yorkshire where he continued his literary studies into a wide variety of topics. It was not too long before he found himself employment in the village of Netherdale as a school teacher. It was within this same community that he met and fell in love with Anna Spence. Aram's quest for knowledge took precedence over everything else, but his new found love seemed to accept this concept of the relationship and supported him. Eugene Aram married Anna, possibly anticipating her full support in every venture into which he entered. But Eugene, although possessing a mass of academic knowledge, had no real idea of responsibility towards his wife. Being neglected, she succumbed to infidelity, which hurt Aram immensely and the couple parted, though he would often call upon Anna and treat the home as his own.

In 1734 Aram visited William Norton, a gentleman friend from Knaresborough who allowed him to stay at his home. Aram digested much of the knowledge contained within Norton's generous library and occasionally acted as a private tutor to the families of the local gentry. His studies included mathematics, Latin, Greek and religious studies but in particular the Pentateuch, which he studied in Hebrew. Aram had created an excellent reputation for himself and probably amassed a fair degree of financial stability from such activities. Certainly he became a most respected member of the community. Yet there still existed an air of aloofness which could have been misconstrued as selfishness. It is certain that Aram was regarded as a conceited individual, a perception which was to cause him many future problems.

The year 1744 saw Eugene return to London in search of his fortune. There he served the Reverend Mr Plainblanc in Piccadilly, as an usher in Latin and writing. Aram returned to Knaresborough in 1745 and continued his studies. Yet a different attitude seemed to be evident to those who knew him; Aram seemed to be more cynical and avaricious. The scholar remained in Knaresborough for a period of time sufficient enough for his avarice to cause him a severe problem. Aram was friendly, socially, with a flax dresser by the name of Richard Houseman who was an amiable sort of chap but of weak character. It would seem that he acted upon Aram's command. One evening the pair met with Daniel Clark, a shoemaker, in Knaresborough. Clark had recently married into a good family and was openly discussing the wealth he was expected to receive via the marriage. After a discussion with Houseman, Aram once again spoke with Clark, and suggested how Clark could use the situation to his advantage. All Clark had to do, he said, was visit local dealers in anything from jewellery to clothing to furniture, explain about his expectations and obtain the valuables on the promise that they would be paid for within a month or so. Clark agreed and bought so much on credit that it was only a matter of time before the dealers and traders caught up with him and demanded payment. The pressure began to play upon Clark's mind. He became paranoid but refused to discuss the problem with anyone else. Clark had obtained a large quantity of valuables by deceit which left him vulnerable to those who knew his secret; namely Aram and Houseman!

Late in the evening of 7th February 1745, Aram, Clark and Houseman met. Aram told both men that a discussion had to take place in relation to Clark's compromising situation. The meeting took place in an upstairs room of Aram's estranged wife's house and lasted for about thirty minutes. Anna Aram was curious as to what was taking place but preferred to ignore the strange gathering. Clark had been instructed to bring the valuables with him in order that the trio could discuss the correct disposal of the property. After the meeting the three men walked through the fields to St Robert's Cave. As they approached the entrance to the cave Eugene Aram clubbed Daniel Clark to death and both men buried the body within the damp soil of the dark cave's recess. The sack full of valuables was taken back to Anna Aram's home, where both men shared it out between them. Anna Aram could no longer contain her curiosity and asked Eugene what was happening. Her inquiry was greeted with a negative response and Anna was ordered to her room by an apparently agitated Eugene. After a short time both men again left the house. Tentatively, Anna Aram came downstairs. When she entered the room where Eugene and Richard Houseman had been, she saw that the ashes within the fire grate had been burning more than expected and the stale smell of burnt clothing filled the air. Anna raked through the ashes and saw the remains of a partially bloodstained handkerchief and some other clothing.

Houseman hid his part of the booty in his rear garden, buried within sacking and there it remained for over a year. Eugene Aram entrusted his to a secret hiding place until he could return to London, which he planned to do within the following forty eight hours. Later that morning, news spread throughout the town that Daniel Clark had gone missing. Anna Aram, upon hearing the tale, at once visited Richard Houseman and accused him and Eugene of doing something to Clark, a claim he vehemently denied. Eugene Aram, having recovered his share of the property returned to London where he sold it to a Jew. He then returned to Piccadilly where he worked as an usher at an academy.

But over the following years Aram was unable to settle in any one place. Certainly he found employment, mainly as a tutor, in Nottingham, London (again), Middlesex (location not confirmed) and finally Kings Lynn. The disappearance of

*In 1745, Eugene Aram and his accomplice took their victim, Daniel
Clark, to St Robert's Cave, Knaresborough. His body was to remain
there, undiscovered for 14 years.*

Daniel Clark was all but forgotten in Knaresborough. The
community perhaps believed that he had absconded because
of his debts and settled elsewhere, but there were those who
believed otherwise, for Anna Aram had made no secret of the
bloodstained handkerchief found within her firegrate on the
night of Daniel's disappearance, and how the man had
actually been within her home earlier that evening!

On 1st August 1758, fourteen years after the event, a
labourer was told by a landowner to dig for stone at Thistle-
hill close to Knaresborough. He had dug down about 18
inches when he found the skeletal remains of a human being.
At once he rushed back to the town to tell of his find. The
authorities remembered the mysterious case surrounding
Daniel Clark and soon the talk was of murder. A coroner's
court was held in order that the correct identity of the body
could be ascertained, though it seems that from the
information available the authorities all but believed it to be
the remains of Clark prior to the inquest commencing. Anna
Aram was called to give evidence and recounted the events
which took place within her home in the late evening and

early morning of 7/8 February 1745. In consequence to this Richard Houseman was brought before the court and asked to explain the accusations. The man was a gibbering wreck, unable to answer any questions without trembling and nervously twitching. His actions were more than suspicious and appeared to one and all to be those of a clearly agitated man with much guilt on his mind. The coroner ordered Houseman to pick up one of the skeletal bones and to examine it. Houseman did as he was asked and suddenly exclaimed, 'This is no more Dan Clark's bone than it is mine!' The court were even more suspicious of this audacious comment and questioned Houseman further, who at once became evasive in his answers. It was obvious that Houseman knew much more than he was prepared to confess to. The authorities were in no mood to allow him the opportunity of collecting his thoughts and so further investigations into a possible murder enquiry were ordered.

Magistrates immediately interviewed Houseman who still seemed reluctant to talk. His sentences lacked cohesion and didn't seem to make sense but eventually he told his inquisitors that late in the evening of 7th February,1745 he had indeed visited Aram's home in the knowledge that Daniel Clark was present there. He further stated that Clark had owed him money and it was his intention to recoup some of this, but he had failed. He further claimed that Aram, Clark and another man (unknown to Houseman) had left the house together and that was the last time he had seen Clark alive and that this was his total involvement in the matter. The statement was taken down in long hand and offered to Houseman for signature of authenticity. But he refused to do so, resulting in the magistrates being so annoyed that they opted to detain him in custody until he reported the events accurately. It was decided that he should be taken to York Castle and held there until further notice!

Guards were instructed to escort Houseman to the castle and it was during the journey that Houseman decided to speak the truth and turn Kings Evidence. He was returned

to the magistrates and re-interviewed, where he finally told
of the fate of the unfortunate Clark. He told them that the
bones upon Thistle-hill were nothing to do with Clark and
gave the precise location of Clark's remains. A subsequent
search revealed the true remains of Daniel Clark and at once
Eugene Aram became a wanted man. The Constables
quickly located Aram in Kings Lynn and escorted him back
to York Castle where he was detained awaiting trial for
murder.

The trial took place at the County Assizes, York on 13th
August 1759. The testimony of Richard Houseman virtually
condemned Eugene Aram and when supported by his
estranged wife's testimony the case was complete. Houseman
had been arraigned and acquitted by virtue of his turning
Kings Evidence. Eugene Aram elected to propose his own
defence, which he did in a most impressive and eloquent
manner. He began by quoting his virtues in life and
explained that such a person as he could not have such evil
within him as to commit murder. He then began to introduce
quite pertinent arguments against the authorities' evidence.

'In June 1757, William Thompson, for all the vigilance
of this place, in open daylight, and double ironed, made
his escape; notwithstanding an immediate enquiry set
on foot, the strictest search, and all advertisement, was
never seen or heard of since. If then Thompson got off
unseen, through all of these difficulties, how very easy
was it for Clark, when none of them opposed him? But
what would be thought of a prosecution commenced
against any one seen last with Thompson?'

It was a pertinent point, except the fact that Aram actually
had a witness claiming that he had witnessed him murder
Clark! But he was not yet finished and was to broach several
other factors which caused some consternation among those
present. Aram then quoted sites where skeletal remains had
been found and made the claim that every hill or field
contains such remains, so why should the remains found in
St Robert's Cave be treated as anything different?

Judge Noel carefully listened to Aram's contentions and during his summing up declared them to be some of the most ingenious pieces of reasoning he had ever heard. The jury, however, had little doubt as to his guilt and thus followed the passing of the sentence of death!

Aram confessed his guilt whilst being visited by two clergymen in his cell at York Castle. He explained his motive as being his suspicion of Clark having unlawful commerce with his wife.

The night before he was to hang, Aram made an unsuccessful attempt at taking his own life. He attempted to sever main arteries in his arm by slashing it close to the elbow and wrist of the left arm. When the gaoler went to escort Aram from his cell upon the morning of his execution he found him almost dead through the loss of blood. Amazingly a surgeon was called for and the wounds treated prior to Aram being escorted to the gallows.

So ended the life of Eugene Aram, eminent scholar, respectable citizen and murderer, executed at York 6th August 1759. After being left to hang for an hour the body was cut down and hung in a gibbet iron in Knaresborough Forest where its putrefying remains stayed for almost twenty years. Many still question the degree of Aram's actual guilt. Perhaps Richard Houseman played a greater role than we will ever know?

THE KILLER FROM
ANGEL COURT

THE winter assizes at Manchester in 1876 saw two brothers, William and John Habron brought to trial on the charge of murder. It was alleged that the brothers had shot and killed Police Constable Cock in Seymour Grove, Whalley Range on the night of 1st August of the same year. The trial had caused quite a sensation as the evidence against the brothers seemed quite weak and a successful prosecution was not anticipated. The public gallery was, as usual, filled to capacity, and overflowing with sympathy for the unfortunate Cock family and the apparently innocent Habron brothers. There was nothing extraordinary about those persons present at the trial, yet sitting amongst them was a diminutive character who resembled a gnome, with white hair, whiskers and bow legs. His appearance was one which could not easily be forgotten! As the trial progressed this man sat listening intently to the evidence for and against. The trial lasted just two days. John Habron was found 'Not Guilty', his brother William 'Convicted' and sentenced to death! This sentence was later commuted to one of life imprisonment, a decision which was later vindicated when the real killer confessed while awaiting execution for another murder.

Charles Frederick Peace was born in Angel Court, Sheffield on 14th May 1832 the youngest of four children to a highly regarded shoemaker. During his adolescent years Charlie was apprenticed to a local rolling mill where he worked long hours for a paltry wage. Whilst at the mill he

Charlie Peace, the diminutive killer of Angel Court, as sketched in court in 1879 by his counsel.

suffered a horrendous accident which was to cause him a disability for the rest of his life. His leg was crushed between some machinery and stock, resulting in serious ligament damage causing him to walk with a permanent limp. He had also suffered an injury to his left hand, losing at least two fingers and much of its mobility. As if these injuries were not sufficient, Peace had also received an injury to his jaw which did nothing for his facial appearance.

Despite these misfortunes, his interest as a young man was that of amateur dramatics and the music hall. Indeed, he was an excellent violinist and was often invited to play at various concerts in the North of England. However, the revenue from such work did not satisfy his craving for money and so he opted for a different career, that of crime! Before reaching the age of twenty he was an experienced petty thief and practised burglar, indeed he incorporated his musical ability into his crimes. Prior to breaking into identified properties Peace would observe the routine of the household by posing as a wandering musician; it is also claimed that within his violin case were concealed all the required tools for housebreaking! Luck deserted Peace as in 1851 he was jailed for one month on a housebreaking charge in Sheffield and three years later he collected a four year sentence for a number of similar crimes which occurred in the Sheffield region. The background for disaster was thus created. Peace was a hardened crook and keen to make money from anything despite its illegality.

In 1859 he met with and married Hannah Ward, a widow with one son. Peace was taken with his partner and one could be excused for believing that he kept his illegal activities secret from her. The couple had two children, one boy, one girl, but Peace knew little about his family as late in 1859 he was jailed after being apprehended attempting to recover booty from the scene of a crime. Perhaps for the first time the awful realisation of Hannah that her husband was not the individual she had expected must have caused her great dismay. Even greater must have been the pressure of losing her husband to a jail sentence of five years. For two years after his release in 1864 he avoided capture during various burglaries, but in 1866 he was caught during such an act in Victoria Park, Manchester. He was sentenced to six years imprisonment under the name of George Parker. However, he was released on 'Ticket of Leave'. This was a pass given to a convict freed from actual confinement upon the conclusion of part of the jail sentence, but there was still a requirement that the released prisoner had to report periodically to designated authorities. He returned to the family environment in Manchester. No doubt pressured by his recent jail term Peace opted to move his family back to the Sheffield area where his activities were not so suspicious and in 1875 the family moved into number 40, Victoria Place, Britannia Road, Darnoll, Sheffield, Peace now elected to attempt to make a decent living for his family by frame-making and hawking his wares, but this may well have been a further tool for him to assess properties ripe for burglary! The family seemed to enjoy their new environment and Charlie in particular became friendly with the Dyson family who resided next door but one in Victoria Place.

Arthur Dyson, a railway construction worker and his wife, Katherine, a tall well built woman, had become close to the Peace family. Certainly, Charlie found Katherine Dyson's company to his liking and with the latter apparently being unhappy with her marital state, the relationship was destined to be a particularly volatile one. The attention which Charlie displayed to Katherine Dyson was quite open. The couple were often seen together and seemed oblivious to local gossip or the feelings of their respective partners. Arthur Dyson confronted Charlie and warned him to stay away from Katherine. However, Katherine often sent Charlie love notes requesting clandestine assignations. Matters came to a head in June 1876 when Arthur Dyson physically confronted Peace and advised him to leave him and his wife alone (Dyson actually stood at 6 foot 5 inches tall with Peace at 5 foot 4 inches!) but Peace ignored his threats and continued to make a nuisance of himself, loitering outside their home at all hours of day and night. Dyson, a placid man by nature, must have been at the end of his tether.

Saturday 1st July of the same year saw another amazing incident transpire in this awful scenario. Peace met Dyson in the street and actually tripped him over before hurling abuse and sauntering off to his own home. Dyson offered no retaliation and seemed resigned to the fact that Peace was a man possessed. Katherine did not take too kindly to the assault and, unlike her husband, elected to voice her opinions upon the street. Later that same evening Peace was returning to his home when he overheard Katherine discussing his immature actions against her husband. She ridiculed Peace in front of the neighbours, any sign of love, lust or other emotion now absent from Peace's former sweetheart. The angry little man rushed towards his former lover and in front of witnesses produced a revolver from his coat pocket and said 'I will blow your bloody brains out, and your husband's too'. As a result of these threatening actions Katherine Dyson informed the local Constables and a warrant for the arrest of Charlie Peace was issued.

But Peace was too wily and at once absconded from the Sheffield region, complete with his family, and removed to Hull, where his mother lived. Later that month they opened a small cafe in Collier Street, Hull.

Back in Sheffield, the Dysons decided to move home, almost certainly in the hope that Charlie Peace would never again darken their door. Their new home was in Banner Cross Terrace, in the opposite side of the city. Thursday 26th October saw the Dyson family actually move homes. Arthur and Kate had just arrived in Banner Cross Terrace and approached the front door of their new abode when suddenly a tiny dark stooping figure appeared from the doorway. It was Charlie Peace! With a smile of contempt upon his face he greeted the Dysons, 'I shall follow you wherever you go and annoy you.' Arthur Dyson reminded him of the existence of the warrant for his arrest, but Peace retorted that such things did not worry him. Over the weeks which followed Charlie Peace could be seen loitering around the Banner Cross Terrace area. True, he made no direct approach to the Dysons but undoubtedly his presence was a great concern to them, especially Arthur.

So the situation continued until Wednesday 29th November 1876, the day after the Manchester trial of the Habron brothers when Charlie Peace again visited Banner Cross Terrace. At approximately 8.00 pm he was speaking to the Dyson's neighbours and making acid comments about Arthur and in particular Katherine's promiscuity and he was later spotted skulking to the rear of the Dyson's home. A short while later Katherine Dyson lit a lantern and ventured into the rear garden en route to the outside lavatory oblivious to the fact that Peace was also in the rear garden. Having completed her task Katherine opened the door of the lavatory and was confronted by Peace complete with revolver in hand. Screaming she rushed frantically back into the toilet and slammed the door closed. Arthur Dyson heard the commotion and came rushing out. He saw the dwarf-like figure of Peace dart down a dark passageway and gave chase. Peace stopped and turned to face Arthur and a brief struggle ensued, resulting in Peace twice shooting Dyson. One of the bullets came to rest in his brain and Arthur Dyson died at 10.30 pm.

Investigating authorities at once issued a description of the man with whom they wished to speak in relation to the crime: 'Thin, slightly built, 55-60 years of age, five feet four inches tall, grey, nearly white hair, beard and whiskers. Bow legged with one or more fingers missing from left hand.' A reward of £100 was offered for information leading to his arrest but Peace had escaped, flitting from area to area. In Hull in 1877 he fired two shots at an innocent householder during a daring burglary.

Peace must have felt supremely confident about evading capture. He was known to have committed further crimes in Oxford and Bristol before settling for a short time in the city of Nottingham. During his stay there he met with a widow by the name of Susan Grey. Peace was soon living with her and remained an active burglar. The local authorities soon identified Peace's modus operandi and were close to arresting him for the local crimes when he again moved on, this time to London at 5 Evelina Road, Peckham. Using the alias of Mr and Mrs Thompson, the couple attended church every Sunday and seemed respectable enough. Peace's real wife (Hannah) soon arrived on the scene and apparently raised no objection to the new relationship – in fact she posed as the couple's housekeeper before leaving for America. Soon a child was born of the relationship between Peace and Susan and to neighbours the family seemed completely respectable. Mr and Mrs Thompson held music evenings within their home, neighbours would come to hear Charlie play his violin and comment upon his natural flair. From his ill-gotten gains

Peace was afforded a few luxuries. He dressed in smart suits and even dyed his hair black (possibly in an attempt to disguise his looks from enquiring Police officers). The transformation was completed by virtue of spectacles and an artistic temperament. Sadly, Peace could not resist the urge to go on stealing and Susan was now drinking heavily and could not be relied upon to maintain her false status. The neighbours began to see through the false front projected by the couple.

In the early hours of Thursday 10th October 1878 at around 2.00 am Police Constable Edward Robinson noticed a light flash from the rear of 2 St John's Park, Greenwich. On approaching the rear of the house, Robinson again observed the light. Suddenly it was extinguished and the Constable saw a man run out of the rear of the house. He at once gave chase. The man being pursued was Charlie Peace who fired three shots at the Constable. One entered Robinson's right arm above the elbow, but the brave officer

Peace's home in Peckham, London in 1878, where Peace lived with his mistress and his wife, who posed as the couple's housekeeper.

managed to overpower Peace and take him to Park Row Police station. Peace gave his name as John Ward and was subsequently tried under this name at the Central Criminal Court (Old Bailey) for attempted murder. He was sentenced to life penal servitude. However, Susan Grey was not to be underestimated. She felt vindictive, and the promise of a £100 reward convinced her to speak to the Police stating that Peace was the killer of Arthur Dyson in Sheffield.

The stage was set in Sheffield. Katherine Dyson was ready to testify, the evidence was heavily stacked against Peace. Curiously, Peace was not afforded the opportunity of being lodged in a Northern prison, but was transferred to and from Pentonville Prison via train. It was on one such journey that a most remarkable incident took place. Peace and two warders (to whom he was handcuffed) had left London on the Sheffield bound train. As the train reached the Yorkshire Border Peace requested a call of nature and was supplied with a brown paper bag. As the warders turned their backs to allow the prisoner some privacy Peace leapt from the carriage window! One warder turning in time to see his prisoner's feet disappearing through the window, instinctively grabbed hold of Peace's foot and refused to let go. It was a remarkable scene, the train powering along the track with Peace hanging upside down from one of the carriage windows. Eventually he managed to wriggle free only to land head first upon the track after initially striking his head upon the carriage foot plate. The train was stopped and both warders ran back to the crumpled form upon the railway line, Peace was unconscious and blood oozed from a gash in his head. The warders carried him back to the train and again handcuffed themselves to the prisoner, having learned from bitter experience that they should not have removed the 'cuffs' for any purpose, let alone to permit a prisoner to urinate!

The train arrived in Sheffield at 9.20 am and great crowds were in attendance to view the remarkable Peace. A Police Surgeon treated his wounds and a special Police Court was assembled at which Peace was committed for trial at Leeds Assizes. On Tuesday 4th February 1879 Charles Frederick Peace was found guilty of murder, the jury taking just fifteen minutes to decide upon their verdict. He was taken to Armley jail, Leeds, to await execution. During this time he was visited by the Reverend J.H. Littlewood to whom Peace confessed all, including the murder of Police Constable Cock at Whalley Range. The execution day soon arrived (Tuesday 25th February 1879) and Peace seemed unnerved by his fate. Of his last meal he is claimed to have stated, 'This is bloody rotten bacon'. The executioner, William Marwood, stated that Peace met his maker with remarkable fortitude, and suffered not upon his fate. His fortitude was displayed by virtue of some memorial cards which Peace had printed before the execution, which stated: IN MEMORY OF CHARLES PEACE WHO WAS EXECUTED IN ARMLEY PRISON. TUESDAY, FEBRUARY 25th 1879. Aged 47. FOR THAT I DON (sic) BUT NEVER INTENDED.

THE WIDOW OF FLAMINSHAW

THIS murder story is set near to the city of Wakefield. Situated to the south of Leeds, Wakefield dates back to Roman times and possesses a fine cathedral church from Norman times, rebuilt around 1392. It was afforded a bishopric in 1880. At one time the city was the largest cloth-producing centre in the West Riding. However, since those days it has expanded and it now looks like so many other modern cities with its new architecture and busy traffic system. Yet for all this much remains to remind us of Wakefield's charm.

Elizabeth Smith was a 67 year old widow who lived close to Wakefield in the community of Flaminshaw at the beginning of the 19th century. Elizabeth had one son who worked and resided in Leeds. She was a well respected woman who was famous for her hard working disposition. Elizabeth would help anyone and was a typical Good Samaritan. Occasionally her goodwill was abused by the odd character but neighbours would rectify matters by persuading the nefarious character to repay or return the favours they had abused. But fate was to play a cruel trick upon Elizabeth. In her latter years she had taken to keeping cows and selling their produce. This had provided her with a reasonable income and provided a comfortable lifestyle. Her son in Leeds was able to lead his own life without having to subsidise his mother; that is until February 1803 when two of Elizabeth's three cows died. So Elizabeth began to struggle financially. It was only a matter of weeks before her position became worsened as her savings disappeared on day to day living. Neighbours were curious when they failed to see Elizabeth during the course of their daily lives. She was usually a creature of habit yet she seemed to have changed her daily routine. Elizabeth's problems were discussed among the local community and a collection was raised by fellow villagers, providing sufficient funds for her to purchase a further cow. Her son in Leeds upon hearing of her traumatic experience forwarded the sum of 18 guineas to purchase a third cow. He advised her to await the arrival of the spring weather before purchasing the cow as the cold of winter could provide further problems to both her and the cows. During the following days Elizabeth bragged about the kindness of her son and discussed her pride in him and his obvious business success in Leeds.

Sadly, loose talk can create great problems. The gratitude shown by Elizabeth Smith was eagerly discussed in local taverns as too the financial support she had received from her son. John Terry and his apprentice Joseph Heald, two local crooks, overheard a discussion of these matters and decided to act upon it. The following is the confessional tale told by John Terry. Its accuracy is, as will later be seen, dubious!

John Terry and Joseph Heald met in a tavern in the early evening. Together they hatched a plot to burgle Elizabeth's home. In order that no suspicion should be held against them they left the tavern separately at around 10.00 pm. They met up again much later at around 1.00 am the following morning and then visited Elizabeth Smith's home. The men quickly found an open window and Terry hoisted Heald into a position where he could climb through and he followed his accomplice by virtue of utilising a large pot as a makeshift step. Once within, the two intruders climbed the stairs and attempted to creep into the unsuspecting woman's room. However, she was disturbed by the noise and awoke to see the men searching through her property. She cried out and leapt out of bed towards the men in an attempt to foil their efforts. Both men kicked and punched the old woman until she was unconscious. Still not satisfied with their work, Heald took a razor and while Terry held her head, Elizabeth Smith's throat was ripped open. Blood spurted everywhere as the carotid artery was sliced open. Heald then took a pair of tongs from the hearth and bludgeoned the old lady's head until both were sure that she was dead. Such a noise had been created that both men left the house without delay, but were sighted by neighbours who had been aroused by the commotion. Terry and Heald had been recognised and were quickly detained by local Constables Shaw and Linley and brought to justice at York. Thus ended Terry's version of events that evening.

In court, Terry was allowed to tell his version of events prior to Heald being present. But once the latter entered the courtroom and heard what his alleged partner was insinuating then matters seemed to change. Heald was seemingly shocked by what he heard and turned to Terry and exclaimed, 'Terry, I thought thou wouldst not have deceived me so, thou knowest I was not with thee!' Terry quite calmly reiterated, 'Thou knowest there is a god above who knows all!' Heald again screamed at Terry to stop telling lies about him, adding, 'Thou had better lay it upon somebody else.' The inference was there for all to hear, but Terry was not to have any of it. Confidently he looked Heald in the eye and said, 'I will not hang an innocent man; thou knowest there were but us two, and god for our witness.' Any loyalty that had existed between the two was no longer evident. The jury were impressed by neither man and found both guilty as charged, and so the death sentence was passed upon John Terry and Joseph Heald, the execution date being Monday 21st March 1803, at York.

Both prisoners remained silent about the case right up to execution day when the Reverend Mr Brown visited Terry in the condemned cell. The prisoner showed remorse for his actions and further told the Reverend that Joseph Heald was innocent of the charge against him! The Reverend refused to

accept such a confession and told him so. After all had the
evidence not been heard at the trial? Terry was now
becoming riddled with guilt and repeated that Heald was
innocent and that his life should be spared. His main worry
was that he was to hang with an innocent man! The
Reverend Brown at once sought an audience with the trial
judge and they discussed Terry's confession. However, his
lordship was not about to be fooled by such tricksters and
refused to change his decision. He believed that Heald's guilt
had been sufficiently proved during the trial. Although he
stated this fact the judge still felt that it was his duty to have
the matter investigated as efficiently as possible and so sent
his marshall, Mr Wells, to speak with both prisoners and to
assess the situation accordingly. Wells could find no reason
to believe Terry and so ordered that the execution take place.

John Terry was the first to emerge from his cell en route
to the gallows. He continually expounded that Heald was
innocent, but like his life, talk was cheap. Terry was clearly
agitated and faltered as he ascended the scaffold. Once upon
the platform he faced the noisy rabble who had come to
witness the event, and said, 'They are going to hang an
innocent man for he is as innocent as any of you!' Upon
making this speech he leapt off the platform and onto the
ladder leading from the gallows but was caught and held by
a clergyman who refused to let go of his waist. Eventually
Terry was literally dragged back onto the gallows and
positioned over the drop. Joseph Heald stood beside him and
seemed resigned to his fate, displaying no sign of nervousness
nor fear of death. Terry was still rambling and again
screamed at the crowd 'It was me that murdered the woman,
I said it was Heald, but I did so to save my own life and
would not any of you hang an innocent man to save your
own life? Don't hang Heald; if you do I shall be guilty of two
murders!'

Once again Terry was re-positioned over the drop and the
noose placed around his neck. As the drop opened Terry
leapt forward and grabbed the scaffold rail. His foot lodged

on the edge of the beam in order that he did not drop into the darkness below and join Joseph Heald who was dangling there. After a struggle Terry was forced to jump into the drop and eternity alongside a man who was possibly innocent.

Was Heald innocent or had Terry spoken the truth to his captors? We shall never know. The evidence for his innocence is rather weak and to this author's mind the only manner in which he could be innocent was if he did not go to Elizabeth Smith's house at all that morning. If he did so, then he is guilty by virtue of being present when murder took place. From the evidence available the correct verdict and sentence was prescribed.

MURDER OF THE
CHIEF OFFICER OF POLICE

ALTHOUGH historically Huddersfield's past can be traced back to Roman times it is essentially a modern town. Situated in the Colne Valley close to the rivers Holme and Calder, it is close to rugged moorland which rises above the town like some oppressive being maintaining a watchful eye upon the inhabitants below.

During the early years of the 19th century, Huddersfield was a bleak town though industrious with its mills providing much of the employment in the community. Its inhabitants displayed the typical Yorkshire friendliness which prevails to this day. Similarly the townsfolk of the 19th century could identify troublemakers or agitators with little trouble, especially so when such persons were strangers to the community. Such a situation transpired early in 1839, when a troublesome wretch by the name of Alexander McLaghlin Smith moved into the Huddersfield region. Smith was 35 years of age and of a particularly volatile disposition. He was residing in the Elland/Halifax region and occasionally worked as a labourer, though his attitude to work did not endear him to many. Smith's main problem appears to have been his liking for alcohol. That in itself is no problem for most, but for Smith it aroused a violent streak within him and should any person so much as look at him in the wrong way then they stood a good chance of being beaten up.

Smith had often spent the night in the cells at Huddersfield prison and was well-known to most of the local Constables who were in the unfortunate position of having to restrain

Advertising for new members of the constabulary in 1848. For the 14 night constables, 17s a week and the use of a great coat or oil skin cape had to be enough for 'all other fees, presents or rewards' were 'prohibited on pain of instant dismissal'.

Smith during his turbulent adventures. However, the Police were aware of Smith's background and were often able to pacify him by talking of his wife and children in Stirling, Scotland, from whom he was separated but still yearned for. Such talk often resulted in Smith becoming emotional, suddenly like a lost lamb searching for comfort and stability. Perhaps then the Police believed that they understood Smith and his methods and therefore perceived no real threat from him. The principles of policing in 19th century England were somewhat different from today's society, but the one task a Police Officer cannot lose sight of is that of professionalism and concentration on the task at hand. The loss of the latter can compromise an officer's position in respect to his safety! And so we move on to the events which transpired on Tuesday 28th April 1840.

It had been a normal day in Huddersfield, no serious incidents requiring police involvement had transpired and the Chief Police Officer of the town, Mr William Duke was one of several officers on duty that day. It was around 4.00 pm when Constable Dawson received information that Alexander Smith was performing in the town, looking for opposition for a punch up. Dawson soon found Smith, and taking hold of him, could smell alcohol upon his breath. Smith was in no mood to come quietly and remonstrated with the Constable. However, after a minor scuffle, Smith succumbed and was taken to Huddersfield prison house. Once inside Smith again became disruptive, screaming threats at the officers within his sight. Dawson took his prisoner into the prison yard and was followed by William Duke. Smith continued his verbal barrage and produced a small pruning knife from his pocket, at which point he lunged at Duke in an unsuccessful attempt to injure him. The knife was knocked from his hand, leg and wrist chains quickly locked upon him and he was then placed in a cell.

During his confinement Smith continued to shout and scream abuse at anyone who would listen. His accusations were not directed solely towards the police but to society in general, as he threatened to kill anyone who came near him. Smith was not usually so obnoxious and it seemed clear that he had not consumed a great quantity of alcohol, yet something was causing him great grief. The protestations continued and Smith began to throw things about his cell. He was not at that time restrained to wall irons but undoubtedly should have been.

Perhaps with this thought in mind, Duke and Constables Dawson and Dalton decided to enter the cell and to speak with Smith in an attempt to pacify him, or failing this restrain him with the wall irons. Duke explained to Smith that he wished to speak with him in order to ascertain what his problem was. Smith agreed through the locked cell door that he would welcome this, and so William Duke instructed that the door be opened in order that he should enter. As the heavy door creaked open Alexander Smith rushed out of the cell directly towards William Duke who stood momentarily motionless as he attempted to grasp what was happening. But it was too late. Smith was clutching yet another pruning knife in his hand and he thrust it into the body of the stationary Duke at which point Duke turned and ran out of the prison, quickly followed by Smith and Dawson. Constable Dalton took to his heels in the opposite direction, not in an attempt to flee but to intercept the prisoner's projected escape route from a different direction. Smith continued to chase the badly wounded Duke around the exterior of the prison and soon caught up with him where he at once began to stab the defenceless officer into submission. Constable Dawson dived upon the attacker in an attempt to save his colleague and he too received laceration injuries to his body. He would have undoubtedly been stabbed to death had it not been for Constable Dalton who drew his staff and brought it crashing down upon Smith's wrist knocking from his hand the offensive weapon which he at once seized. Smith was restrained with the assistance of some townspeople. Further officers attended and secured Smith to a cell wall with double chains.

Doctor Wrigley was summoned and at once attended to the injured officers. William Duke was in a terrible state. He lay in a pool of his own blood which was flowing from various severed arteries in his body. The doctor's attempts to stem the flow were insufficient to say the least as there was a multitude of possibly fatal lacerations and puncture wounds. Duke looked up to the doctor and said 'Don't remove me, doctor, don't be so cruel – let me die here!' The doctor, of course, was duty bound to make every effort to save Duke's life and so had him removed to his home nearby where his wounds were washed and treated. But sadly within ten minutes he died from his wounds.

From within his cell Alexander Smith was heard to scream disgust at having injured only two people. He further claimed that he would have hurt more had he been given the opportunity and furthermore he complained because he had cut his own hand during the attack!

An inquest took place the following day, Wednesday 29th April at the George Inn. Alexander Smith was conveyed to the inn in an open carriage. To the digust of the whole town he was still wearing the blood of William Duke and Constable Dawson upon his clothes and hands. Smith seemed to enjoy the attention his butchery had caused and some claimed that there was the glimmer of a smile upon his face as he looked from the carriage. Smith was brought before the coroner, Mr Thomas Dyson and the facts of the case discussed. With this completed, the coroner asked Smith if he had anything which he wished to say. (This was often an opportunity for the defendant to show remorse for his sins.) But Smith callously replied, 'Me ask any question? Are you satisfied with what you have got? Then be doing!' Smith's reprehensible attitude did little to deter from his already precarious situation and it came as no surprise when the jury, who themselves displayed no emotion towards Smith, returned a verdict of 'Wilful Murder'. Smith was then conveyed to York Castle to await trial at the Summer Assizes in the town. En route for Huddersfield he was jeered and suffered verbal abuse but nothing to the extent to which he perhaps deserved. The local populace were dignified in their distaste towards his abhorrent behaviour and proved themselves to possess remarkable restraint considering the ill feeling against the killer. During the journey to York Castle one of the gaolers asked Smith if he felt saddened by his affairs, but once again the prisoner proved himself to be most arrogant as he explained that he felt no more sorrow for killing policemen than he did for killing bullocks! Perhaps evil is too kind an adjective for this individual!

During his confinement in York Castle, Smith found himself ostracised. Even his fellow inmates found it difficult to talk to or trust him. He was one to avoid. It was now that the real pressures of what had occurred in Huddersfield forced themselves upon him as the tense environment of York Castle brought home the stark reality of the situation in which he now found himself. But Smith was unable to comprehend the difference between right and wrong. His mind had taken control of its own thoughts and emotions

Huddersfield County Borough Police Force's first police station, situated at the corner of Victoria Street and Bull and Mouth Street.

and Alexander Smith was not in total control of anything he did. To put it simply, he was undoubtedly insane. Over the weeks which followed, his mental condition deteriorated to such an extent that he was secured in a safe cell for his own safety.

Alexander Smith was brought to trial at York on the 21st July 1840, Mr Baron Rolfe presiding over matters. The result was hardly surprising; Smith was found guilty but insane, and so was detained during Her Majesty's pleasure.

It may well be that Smith was in control of his actions on the 28th of April 1840 but there seems much evidence to indicate that the pressures of his actions that day had altered his state of mind to a condition from which he could not recover. Perhaps as such this would have been an escape from the living hell which Smith must have endured thereafter.

THE BODY IN THE
GORSE BUSHES

MARITAL bliss is something which many strive to achieve. But human nature being what it is, for some people 'the grass is always greener on the other side of the fence.' Sexual encounters are often sought with little thought as to the possible outcome or heartache these may cause to the individuals concerned or those indirectly involved. To destroy a healthy close relationship can be equated with destroying a whole life. The memories of both good and bad times and the sense of real trust and honesty can suddenly disappear, causing despair and animosity and the end of the relationship. Sexual encounters outside the bounds of marriage are nothing new. They have taken place for hundreds of years and caused as much grief then as they do now. But some actually caused more dramatic actions from those involved, including murder!

In the mid 18th century, John Robinson, 33 year old farmer, owned much of the land in the area of Mickleby, near Whitby, North Yorkshire. Such wealth afforded him great respect from the local community especially as he was one of the main employers in the area. Robinson was noted for his caring attitude towards the poor and the homeless and was often seen to provide food from his land for these unfortunate souls. Robinson was very much the provider and the local community the recipients. Those who were fortunate enough to gain employment on his land were permitted to utilise small amounts of the crops for their own purposes. These were excellent man-management tactics and inspired the labourers to work that extra bit harder in order to reap the benefits of the land while simultaneously increasing the profits Robinson would receive. Not only had Robinson a happy working environment but his personal lifestyle seemed idyllic. Married with four children he appeared to be the perfect husband and father while his affluent position allowed him to spend as much time as he deemed necessary with his family whom he seemed to adore.

Susannah Wilson was an ex-employee of the Robinson household. She had been a very efficient and highly thought of maid servant. She had left the household under somewhat mysterious circumstances, announcing her departure just hours before she actually left. Mrs Robinson was rather perturbed at the loss of such a good maid servant but Susannah could not be persuaded to remain. Instead she went to stay with friends in Guisborough. Mrs Robinson's suspicions as to the cause of the sudden departure of Wilson were founded upon woman's intuition. Her husband refused to discuss the matter in any depth with her and immediately set about employing another maid. But village gossip was rife as news of Susannah's departure spread through the taverns and inns like wildfire. There had been much speculation about a sexual relationship between master and maid but no one had believed it. Suddenly all the idle gossip seemed to fit together like pieces of a jigsaw and scandal erupted in a sleepy North Yorkshire town!

It seemed that the only person who did not know of the relationship was Robinson's wife who as lady of the manor was not privy to such gossip – and certainly not as one of the injured parties! Susannah Wilson left her friends' Guisborough home one spring morning, informing them that she was to meet John Robinson who had promised her a bushel of wheat. Before leaving she spoke of a fear that she held and said that if anything odd should happen to her or she should suffer any injury then John Robinson should be the subject of an investigation.

It was around twelve miles from Guisborough to Mickleby

and Wilson did not seem too concerned as she set out to walk the distance. Meanwhile that same day at Robinson's farm, John Robinson had performed his normal managerial duties and late in the afternoon informed the household that he was going to Staithes and would spend the night there with friends. He left around 5.00 pm bidding his family the usual caring goodbyes. At around 7.00 pm that evening he met with Susannah Wilson who was waiting for him at a pre-arranged location upon his land. The couple walked together and discussed their predicament. Certainly Robinson had more to fear than Susannah Wilson and one might feel that she could justifiably blackmail him, but the farmer was not in the best psychological state to listen to what she had to say. He now wished to rid himself of the problem which he had created, and the situation had worsened by virtue of the fact that Susannah had told him that she was with child, his child!

John Robinson wilfully led Wilson to an area which he had previously visited, an area which was perfect for murder! Sitting down with the ex maidservant he lulled her into a false sense of security and made an excuse to leave her for a few seconds. During this time he collected an axe which he had hidden at that location for precisely this reason. He then felled the girl with one swift blow of the weapon which split open her skull causing immediate death. In a frenzied attack he continued to beat Susannah Wilson's corpse with the axe until it was barely recognisable, his temper and disgust at the girl was so great. Having gained control of his actions Robinson suddenly realised the consequence of his crime so he then tasked himself with placing the body in a location where it would not be found. A thick gorse bush close to the scene seemed the ideal location as the area was secluded and it seemed unlikely that anyone would ever have cause to visit it. So the remains of Susannah Wilson were left to decompose in the inclement spring weather. In order to substantiate his alibi, Robinson then proceeded to Staithes where he arrived at about 9.30 pm. He remained the night and returned to his farm the following morning.

It was some five weeks later when the rumours of Susannah Wilson's disappearance emerged. The friends from Guisborough were concerned as to her welfare as they had not heard from her since she left for Mickleby. Enquiries were made with John Robinson and his household but the farmer denied ever meeting the maidservant and promptly produced his alibi, saying he spent the night at Staithes. These lies were initially accepted as being the truth and there was discussion amongst Wilson's friends and the authorities that she may have gone elsewhere and moved completely from the environment, especially so if she had been pregnant. As it stood it was nothing but conjecture that Robinson was her lover and that he had done away with her. Returning to the farmer the authorities requested that they be permitted to carry out a thorough search of his land in case Susannah had suffered a fatal accident. Robinson had no alternative but to grant such a request. Dozens of local people, including the male members of the Robinson household participated in the search which took several hours to carry out. How Robinson must have fretted over the fact that his victim lay in the fields now being searched, he may well have wished that he had hidden the remains in a more secret place or even buried them. Yet there was every possibility that they would not be found! That possibility disappeared when news spread that a body had been located in a gorse bush in a remote field but due to its state of decomposition it was difficult to declare its identity. But within minutes of it being viewed by the friends from Guisborough it was identified as Susannah Wilson.

John Robinson was arrested and taken to York castle where he later confessed to the crime and was subsequently hanged, with his remains later given to local surgeons for the purpose of dissection.

In this unhappy tale great sympathy must be felt for the surviving members of the Robinson family who must have been inconsolable in their realisation that their husband and father was in fact a fraud, a man who had fallen victim to his own lust and desire. There are those who will say that John Robinson was not solely to blame and that such sexual encounters do in fact take two consenting partners. But could anyone really fault Susannah Wilson for succumbing to her employer's instructions and attentions. Indeed, was there really any alternative for her? Most certainly the victim in this case cannot have been totally unaware of the dangers presented to her when she arranged the assignation with her ex master and lover. Yet something forced her to attend despite such obvious risks. Some people believe that she intended to blackmail Robinson. If this was the case then perhaps it was a case of villain killing villain!

THE CASE OF THE IRISH HAWKERS

THE market town of Mirfield stands on the river
Calder on the Dewsbury to Huddersfield road,
approximately five miles to the north east of Huddersfield. It is here that the striking house named 'Roe Head'
(once a school) was used by the immortal Bronte sisters. Emily
wrote three poems here and Anne was to later return to the
community as governess of Blake Hall, where she structured
the storyline of *Agnes Grey*. Local legend also claims that a
site located approximately half a mile from the town was
where the legendary Robin Hood drew his last breath!

Mirfield, like so many of its counterparts is a proud
community. There is nothing which instantly differentiates
this town from any other until one mentions the name 'Water
Royd House', known locally as the 'Murder House'. For in
the early days of summer 1847, three members of this one
household were quite literally butchered.

James Wraith, a 77 year old local joiner / builder / handy-
man and his 67 year old wife, Ann, together with local
servant girl, 21 year old Caroline Ellis, resided at Water
Royd House. The Wraiths were comfortably off for both
owned several properties in the Yorkshire area which they
sub-let to various tenants. It was a well-known fact that the
couple had much in the way of financial resources. James
Wraith had begun life as a hard working joiner and built up
his business throughout the years. By 1847 he was in a
situation where he could relax and enjoy his remaining years
without the pressures of finding work. Indeed he often found

Water Royd House today. In 1847, this was the front of the house, where little Joshua made the terrible discovery of his Great Uncle's death.

work for many of his relatives who also lived locally.

Wednesday, May 12 1847 was not dissimilar to any other day in the West Riding parish of Mirfield. The spring of that year had been remarkably warm and the rainfall had been dramatically below the accepted minimum. But things were looking better for the skies were filled with thick black thunder clouds promising a good downpour of rain. The air grew humid and shortly before midday the first rumble of thunder could be heard rolling around the skies.

James Wraith called to speak with his 12 year old great nephew, Joshua Green, and asked him to call at Water Royd House after lunch as he required his assistance with some work. The young boy was only too pleased to help and agreed to his great uncle's request, whereupon James Wraith then returned home before the heavens opened upon him. Sadly, it was to be his last ever journey into the town and the last request he would make of Joshua.

At around 1.30 pm Joshua Green arrived at Water Royd House and as usual he ran round to the rear of the house and attempted to open the kitchen door. Curiously, he found it to be locked and peering through a kitchen window he could not see the key on the reverse side of the lock and wondered if his great uncle James had in fact gone out. Impatiently, he knocked upon the kitchen door, but receiving no reply, he made his way to the front of the house, peering through windows in an attempt to see some form of movement from within. By now the young boy's curiosity had turned into suspicion and worry. These were proved to be well-founded when he arrived at the front door, for beneath the old wooden door he saw blood trickling out onto the stone steps! Horrified, he fled back to his own house where he frantically blurted out his findings to his mother. Mrs Green immediately rushed round to the Kings Head Inn and told the landlord, Mr McKinnell, of her son's find and begged for his assistance. McKinnell ran directly to Water Royd House and managed to force open the front door. The horrific scene which greeted him within was enough to turn any man's stomach; it was absolute carnage.

The body of the servant, Caroline Ellis, lay upon the floor. She had apparently been bludgeoned to death, her skull split open like a ripened horse chestnut, brain matter oozing from the gaping wounds in her head. Her teeth lay on the floor like tossed dice, either knocked out or deliberately extracted by her attacker and her jaw was badly disfigured and obviously smashed. But more horrendous was the fact that her attacker had also slit her throat, severing the carotid artery and pools of blood covered much of the floor and flowed out beneath the foot of the front door.

McKinnell's eyes searched for a route beyond this scene of devastation. He carefully stepped over the body and ventured further into the house. He had not gone much further when he found the body of Ann Wraith lying in the passage close to the parlour and kitchen, blood pouring from the elongated gash in her throat. Her skull had similarly been battered with some kind of heavy object, her right eye had been wrenched from its socket by repeated blows upon the head and face and dangled there like a pocket watch on a chain! The unfortunate McKinnell must have been in total shock at finding such atrocities. Indeed, he must have been unsure as to whether the killer was still within the house yet he continued his search.

McKinnell entered the parlour and found the third and final member of the household. James Wraith lay there, his throat torn open and his skull smashed. So deep was the cut to his throat that his head had almost completely been severed from his body! Laid upon his chest was a possible clue, an open cut throat razor, smeared in blood and clearly bearing James Wraith's name upon its handle. Wraith's trouser pockets had been turned out and close to his body lay a distorted and heavily bloodstained kitchen poker which was approximately two feet long and weighed four pounds. In the kitchen was the remains of the family's lunch, the unconsumed pie, bread and beer still upon the table. The killer had clearly disturbed the household during their midday meal.

A message was sent to the local Constable but by the time he reached the murder scene dozens of local folk had trampled over the site removing objects as keepsakes and morbid souvenirs. The crime scene was no longer sterile, but the use of forensic evidence in 1847 was unheard of, and most clues or evidence there were somewhat obvious to even the untrained eye, though landlord McKinnell had preserved the scene as best he could and did maintain possession of the items he had found.

The town gossip was rife and it was not too long before they had a suspect, an Irish hawker by the name Michael McCabe. Various people told how they had observed McCabe going to Water Royd House at the estimated time of the crime. Without further delay the 35 year old Irishman was arrested. McCabe had been living in the area for upwards of five years and was known to have a liking for money. But for all this he seemed a straightforward sort of person who worked hard to earn his living. When questioned about the crime he seemed to be evasive and did not appear to understand the seriousness of the circumstances leading to his present predicament.

McCabe told the investigating authorities that when he visited the murder house at around 1.00 pm on 12th May he had knocked upon the front door and received no reply. Reluctant to leave without a sale he again rapped upon the door and this time the door edged open a few inches revealing a 'tall handsome man'. The stranger in the house explained that he had no desire to purchase anything but seemed rather nervous and agitated in his manner. McCabe bid the man good day and as he turned to walk away glanced down at the floor and saw blood. The stranger noticed McCabe's anxious look and quickly shut the door on him.

Any normal person seeing such a scene would have reported it immediately to the Constable but not Michael McCabe. He claimed that he did not report his suspicions for fear of reprisal by the local community who, he claimed, had a tendency to mistrust hawkers and there were those who naturally disliked him anyway. So he just left the house and claimed to have continued his business. McCabe went to the home of Charles Flint, a dealer in McCabe's wares. Flint was not at home but McCabe decided to wait until he returned as he required some money in advance. Charles Flint returned home with the news of the horrific murder at Water Royd House still ringing in his ears. He began to tell McCabe of the news and was shocked by the hawker's response. McCabe told Flint that he had visited the murder house earlier that day and during this visit had seen certain things which he was not prepared to discuss. Flint attempted to elicit further information from his visitor but found McCabe reluctant to discuss the matter any further. Flint even gave the hawker the advance he requested, but received no further information pertaining to what McCabe had witnessed at Water Royd House. Once McCabe had left, Flint, whose suspicions had been roused, sent a private message to Constable Howarth about the serious suspicions he held about McCabe's involvement in the crime. Howarth ascertained McCabe's whereabouts and requested a local colleague, Constable Leadbetter to arrest him.

After his arrest McCabe was taken to Dewsbury Police station where he was interviewed and told the same story to Superintendent Richard Green. The senior officer attempted to glean a more accurate description of the stranger within the house, but the only further pointer McCabe could give was an approximate estimation of the man's age, being about 26-28 years. Green quite obviously found McCabe's story too flimsy. He questioned why he had not taken any reporting action when quite clearly he had possibly interrupted someone in the act of doing something extremely suspicious. McCabe's response was more pathetic than anyone could have imagined for he claimed that he felt no real suspicions as it was probable that the family were slaughtering some of their poultry indoors, hence the blood! Despite further reasoning with the prisoner the Police found that McCabe stuck with this same story. It seemed that in all probability he was the killer, although the evidence to support this fact was anything but overwhelming.

But it was not too long before further suspicion was raised against the prisoner, as it was revealed that after visiting Charles Flint, McCabe had returned home and discussed the tragic events at Water Royd House with his wife and apparently had asked her what she would think if it was he who had murdered the household! This statement seemed damning. Why should an innocent man ask such a question? As the interview progressed so McCabe's memory seemed to recall further factors pertaining to the case. He explained that he had previously seen the man who opened the door to him and that he lived in the locality and used some of the local inns. McCabe supplied a more detailed description of the individual which was at once recognised as being similar to Patrick Reid, a 25 year old Irish hawker who tended to reside with the gypsy folk and whose family lived at Dawsgreen, an area predominantly frequented by travelling people. Reid's father was running a type of lodging house in

Dawsgreen and it did not take too long for the authorities to confirm that Patrick was living at home with his father.

With McCabe already in custody there was an obvious belief that he may have been in collusion with Reid and so the Police deemed it necessary to arrest the latter and question him about his alleged role in the crime. Due to the anti-authoritarian feeling which existed among the gypsy folk and the Police during that period it was decided to enter the Reid home in the early hours of the morning when there would be less risk of a volatile situation. Patrick Reid was found asleep in a bedroom with his wife. He created little objection to the arrest but asked if anyone else had been taken into custody! Reid was then taken directly to Dewsbury Police station. The Police made it quite obvious to the two prisoners that they may both be implicated in the crime unless a cast iron alibi could be proved. McCabe was asked if he could identify the stranger in the Wraith household, but on being confronted with Reid he refused to do so, which did little to enhance his innocence. Reid was removed to the Wakefield House of Correction where he was held pending further evidence and trial. Although he admitted to being at the house close to the time of the crime, there was very little else at that point which the Police could prove.

Held at the Kings Head Inn, the inquest seemed quite a straightforward affair, one Hannah Hallas testified to witnessing McCabe in the direct vicinity of the house. Police officers gave an early type of forensic evidence, explaining that blood had been found upon one of McCabe's socks! Another officer detailed precisely what valuables had been removed from the house; two watches, James Wraith's silver one and his wife's gold one, plus about £40 in cash. The missing money gave the Police reason to believe that the killer must have known his prey and their movements for the missing money was kept in a drawer which was secured by a lock and James Wraith generally carried the key on his person. However, such excellent evidence was lost on the case, for none of the stolen items were recovered from either McCabe or Reid, thus casting doubt over their guilt. The local press had already voiced their opinions as to the perpetrator of the crime. Michael McCabe was castigated within the pages of many newspapers, his poor evidence was conclusive proof to them that he must be guilty. Furthermore the motive for the murder was claimed to be theft and being caught in the act! Journalistic licence and trial by press were options which the newspapers during this period often utilised.

Meanwhile back at the inquest Mary Lockwood and Benjamin Morton both gave evidence that they had witnessed Patrick Reid at the house around lunchtime on the day of the murder. This was later clarified as being around 12.30 pm. The Police told how Caroline Ellis had been wearing green garters at the time of her death, one of which was missing. A green material (possibly from a garter) was found at McCabe's house. However, after an examination by a local manufacturer it was confirmed that the materials did not match.

A great nephew of James Wraith, Wraith Green, aged 19 years, gave testimony and explained how some five to six weeks prior to the murder, Patrick Reid had visited Water Royd House and during this he had accused Caroline Ellis of stealing a tea caddy from his basket of wares. So vociferous was the altercation that Wraith was forced to fetch his great uncle to split the parties up. James Wraith had confronted Reid and ordered him off his property with a warning never to return. Prior to leaving Reid was claimed to have screamed at Ellis, 'I will have my revenge upon you.' Rose Hallas gave evidence which tended to confirm this point. Reid had apparently told her of the argument and had threatened that he would get his own back on Caroline Ellis. Suddenly the balance of evidence seemed to swing against Patrick Reid rather than Michael McCabe who still seemed bewildered by his circumstances. Constable Howarth told how he had searched the well to the rear of the Water Royd

House, during which he had recovered a soldering iron and a key. The latter was identified as the missing kitchen door key which the killer must have dumped when fleeing from the house. McCabe was then called to give evidence. He could not identify any new points of evidence and so both prisoners were remanded in custody and the inquest adjourned.

Upon the next inquest hearing, held at Dewsbury Magistrates Court on 5th June 1847 some new evidence came to light, albeit inconclusive. Thomas Kilty, an acquaintance of Patrick Reid and also an Irish hawker, told of a soldering iron used by Reid. It was, he claimed, possibly the same one found in the well at Water Royd House! Further witnesses placed Reid and McCabe at the house, but none could positively link both men as associates or with the crime, yet at a similar third inquest, both were accused of wilful murder! Both men were committed for trial at York but the evidence against both was so weak that the Home Secretary, Sir George Grey, offered a £100 reward to any person who could provide direct evidence to link and convict the men.

The trial commenced at York Assizes on 19th July 1847 and was for the murder of James Wraith only. Michael McCabe had turned Kings Evidence against Patrick Reid once he realised that he was in a desperate position and possibly facing death. Reid was defended by Mr Digby Seymour and he immediately went for McCabe's jugular vein, asking him when exactly he had informed his solicitor that the man who opened the door of Water Royd House to him had been Patrick Reid. McCabe explained that it was either the 19th or 20th of June which was quickly followed by the comment that he had not at that time known of the reward offered by the Home Secretary, thus dispelling such accusations by Seymour. When asked about his visit to the murder house he reiterated the same story as told to Flint and the Police but added that he may have believed one of the family to be ill and that the person opening the door could have been a local doctor or surgeon. Seymour soon discredited much of McCabe's testimony, casting serious doubts over his credibility. Once again he commenced his verbal onslaught upon McCabe, this time asking why he had not before identified Reid, why he had failed to notify the authorities of the strange circumstances perceived at the house, and questioning the stupid comments made to his wife about the murders! McCabe attempted to claw his way out of this verbal assault explaining that he had not wished to expose a fellow who lived locally and thus create animosity. He further confirmed that had he informed the Police of the situation and had he identified Reid prior to being convinced that something nefarious had occurred, then he would be inviting trouble for himself. Hence he added that he had not felt too suspicious about what he perceived on his visit to the house. It was a direct answer and one which left Seymour with few options of attack.

The summing up of the case took some five hours between Seymour and Mr Justice Whightman. The jury retired for a further three hours only to throw the case into utter confusion. Upon returning the spokesman handed Justice Whightman a note which read: if the prisoner be acquitted of the murder of James Wraith may he afterwards be put on trial for the murders of the two women? Justice Whightman ordered that they answer the case in question, and so they returned five minutes later with a verdict of 'Not Guilty'.

A further trial took place on the 20th December, this time before Mr Justice Patterson, again at York. The initial day of the trial was as uneventful as the previous hearings with nothing conclusive coming to the fore. The second day began on a quite different note when 12 year old Mary Hallas gave evidence claiming that she had seen both McCabe and Reid together at Water Royd House on the day of the crime with their baskets of wares in their hands. At last it seemed that real evidence was coming to light. However, all such thoughts were quickly dismissed when it was revealed that McCabe could not hold his basket in his hands as it had no handle and he normally carried it upon his head. Furthermore another witness placed Mary Hallas elsewhere at the time in question.

A convicted horse thief was next called to give evidence. This individual had been in detention with Reid and related how Reid had told him that both he and McCabe were guilty of the murders, having planned the burglary about a month prior to the actual crime! The governor of York Castle was next in the witness box. He explained that during Reid's detention at the castle the prisoner had asked if his circumstances were dire. The governor had informed him that murder was a serious offence and that in all probability if found guilty he would hang. The governor further stated that Reid had then confessed the whole crime to him, reiterating that he had worked without the assistance of anyone. Mr Digby Seymour attempted to find loopholes in this evidence but largely failed to do so.

McCabe's defence was more obvious. The witnesses who had erred whilst giving evidence were identified, plus a most pertinent factor was brought to light. If McCabe had stolen the £40 from the Wraith house, then why did he later go to the home of Charles Flint and ask for a cash advance! Mr Justice Patterson was clear and concise in his summing up. He destroyed the claims of Digby Seymour relating to a man being tried twice for the same crime; Reid had been found innocent of the murder of James Wraith but notwithstanding this fact, he could still have murdered Caroline Ellis. Although the summing up was fair, there was still an air of expectancy for the previous trial had caused some embarrassment in the British judicial system and the press had had a field day with their criticism of Mr Justice Whightman. The jury retired and returned 2½ hours later with a verdict of 'Guilty' against both men. Mr Justice Patterson sentenced both men to death by hanging, and it seemed a fitting and fair end to a long and largely ridiculous trial. However, the drama did not end there, for now it was revealed that Mr Digby Seymour held in his pocket a written confession to the crime by Patrick Reid.

McCabe and Reid were placed in the condemned cell at York Castle, where they were in infamous company with Dick Turpin, who had awaited his end there, a century earlier.

Within this same confession was the exoneration of Michael McCabe. With this knowledge upon him, Seymour had still attempted to have a possibly innocent man found guilty of murder and hanged!

At York Castle, McCabe and Reid were placed in the condemned cell. McCabe was heard to plead with Reid to confess again and thus free him from suspicion. The news he eagerly awaited arrived on the 29th day of December 1847, the death sentence had been revoked. Patrick Reid was again interviewed by McCabe's solicitors and he gave them the facts just as they had occurred that fateful day in early May. He had gone to the house with the intent of stealing valuables. Entering the kitchen he met Caroline Ellis and spoke to her. Taking out his soldering iron he struck her on the back of the head. She screamed and ran to the front door, but before she could open it he was behind her and again struck her on the head. James Wraith was coming out of the coal cellar carrying a pot of beer. Once again Reid used the soldering iron to smash in his head. The blow was so fierce that it broke the iron from its handle. Ann Wraith rushed to see what all the commotion was about and was also struck down with the metal part of the iron. Reid then ran into the kitchen where he saw the poker and returning to the injured persons, he continued to smash the poker down onto their skulls until they offered no further resistance. At this point he stole a gold ring from James Wraith's finger. Suddenly there was a knock at the door. It was McCabe. Reid answered the door and got rid of him. After quickly carrying out a search of the house and stealing the money etc, Reid found James Wraith's razor and one by one slit his victims' throats to ensure that they were silenced forever. Upon leaving the house, he locked the rear kitchen door and threw the key and his soldering iron down the well in the rear garden.

Patrick Reid was hanged at York Castle at approximately 12.15 pm on Saturday 8th of January 1848. Thousands of people witnessed his execution which was an embarrassment for hangman Mr Howard. The noose around Reid's neck was too loose and instead of breaking his neck, the noose merely strangled the killer, thus causing him a slow painful death. It is claimed that his body twitched for up to two hours before finally expiring! Michael McCabe was sentenced to transportation for life as Mr Justice Patterson still believed that he was somehow implicated in the crime. Innocent or not, had McCabe told the truth from the outset, then one may presume he would have been totally exonerated of any implication or involvement in this heinous crime.

A large stone memorial stands in front of the Baptist Zion Chapel and etched upon it is the inscription; 'In memory of Caroline Ellis, aged 21 years, Daughter of George and Jemima Ellis of this parish, who with James Wraith, Gent., and Ann his wife, her master and mistress comprising a whole family was most barbarously murdered at Mid-Day AD· 1847 at Water Royd House, situated 127 yards N.E. from this place.' The monument was erected by the people of Mirfield by subscription.

THE YORKSHIRE WITCH

YORKSHIRE has quite a history of witchcraft. Perhaps the most famous covern was that at Timble to the west of Harrogate. The Timble Witches were revered by many inhabitants of North Yorkshire in the mid 17th century. George Calvert of Kirkbymoorside wrote of witches in 1823, 'these women cast many an evil spell and charm and were held in great fear by a great many good and peaceful folk.' Over the years Yorkshire had a great many legendary witches, Nanny Howe of Kildale and the Ling Bob Witch of Yeadon (Hannah Green), but perhaps the witch most associated with the county has to be Mary Bateman, who is actually referred to as 'The Yorkshire Witch'.

Mary Bateman was born in 1768 at Aisenby, near Thirsk. Her father was a reputable farmer. In 1780 at the tender age of twelve she was sent to work as a servant girl for local gentry in Thirsk, but she was dismissed after being suspected of petty pilfering. She was then placed in employment in York but again within a year she was forced to move on, having been suspected of a serious breach of her employers' trust. Mary fled to Leeds, leaving behind all of her clothing and personal effects including wages! In Leeds she was able to find employment as a dressmaker, a position which she successfully held for three years when she met with a wheelwright by the name of John Bateman. After a three week courtship, she married him in 1792. The couple had initially seemed content with their life, but within weeks of the marriage Mary had commenced her fraudulent lifestyle by obtaining monies from neighbours by deceit. Through such nefarious activities the couple were forced to move residence on several occasions in order to remain one step ahead of the aggrieved parties. John Bateman began to regret marrying Mary who most certainly was not the woman he had believed her to be. To escape from her he joined the supplementary militia, thus leaving her to fend for herself. The year 1799 saw Mary Bateman take up residence in Marsh Lane, Leeds where she commenced her so-called dealings with the supernatural. It seems incredible that anyone could have fallen for the rather pathetic manipulation she manifested upon her victims, the first of which was a Mrs Greenwood. Mary told the woman that her husband was in a serious predicament and that he was about to be accused of a serious crime for which he would receive punishment, that being death! Mary added that should she inform her husband of the situation then matters would worsen. There was just one way in which Mrs Greenwood could save her husband; she had to give Mary Bateman four pieces of gold, four pieces of leather and blotting paper and four brass screws. Mrs Greenwood had no gold to give to Mary and told her so. Mary promptly told her to steal some!

The Greenwood farce was quickly followed by successful dealings with a Mrs Stead whose husband was in the army. The unfortunate woman was told by Bateman that her husband was having an affair with another woman and was about to commit himself to her and leave Mrs Stead. Bateman explained that she could remedy the situation by contacting a Mrs Moore a mystic with whom she was on close terms. (Undoubtedly this woman never existed.) Mrs Stead was advised to bring three half crowns to Mary and to place two pieces of coal upon the front doorstep of her rival's home. Naturally Mrs Stead was ecstatic when her husband remained faithful, and she never realised that the whole scenario was a fabrication of Mary Bateman's imagination. The gullible Mrs Stead was to suffer further from the claims of Mary Bateman, for she was later informed that her father-in-law intended to murder her 'as he disliked her'. However, the mystical Mrs Moore had advised that should Mrs Stead provide Mary with a guinea then all such attempts would be cancelled out by use of her powers. Mrs Stead provided the payment and was now becoming a psychological wreck which provided Mary with further opportunities to obtain monies from her. After being told that her eight year old daughter was to be seduced and ruined, Mrs Stead must have felt that there was a curse upon the family! She again accepted Mary Bateman's terms (seventeen shillings) and was again relieved to be told that Mrs Moore had been able to prevent the incident. A further approach relating to obtaining her husband's discharge from the services caused Mrs Stead to sell furniture and household goods to subsidise the needs of Mrs Moore. Eventually the pressures forced upon her by Mary drove her to suicide. Mrs Stead threw herself into the river Calder to escape her living hell, making her indirectly the first victim of Mary Bateman.

Displaying little or no sympathy for her victims, Mary continued to trick people into giving her money. It is claimed that on one occasion after a massive fire in Leeds in which many people were made homeless, she had walked the streets begging for money and blankets to provide the homeless – naturally none of the goods received were ever forwarded to the needy or homeless. There was nothing that she would not do for financial reward. But she must have been very plausible because the next family to which she attached herself were two Quaker sisters by the name of Kitchen who carried out a linen drapers business close to St Peter's Square, Leeds. The sisters were very close, yet Mary Bateman managed to ingratiate herself with them to such a degree that she became their closest friend and adviser. Once again Mary spun the story that she possessed mystical powers and could forsee future incidents in people's lives, and once again the victims believed her. In September 1803 the younger of the Kitchen sisters took ill. Mary Bateman provided medicines which she claimed had come from a country doctor. The medicines were of no use and within a few days the patient died. The girl's mother arrived from Wakefield and was deeply upset by the circumstances of her daughter's death, yet she held no suspicions of Mary Bateman who had now taken control of the household chores including the preparation of meals. Within a few days Mrs Kitchen and her surviving daughter died and all three were buried in the same grave. Mary Bateman now took control, clearing the Kitchen family home of all of its desirable goods, refusing to allow anyone else access to the home, claiming that the deaths were due to the plague and that it was unsafe to enter until she had it fumigated. The house was almost emptied with Mary assuming the right of ownership and providing for her own home.

It was not too long before Mary resumed her deceitful ways which were providing her with a substantial income. Her psychic reputation had grown and many citizens of Leeds and surrounding areas flocked to her, seeking the assistance of Mary's friend, the mysterious Mrs Moore or her assistant Miss Blythe. In the spring of 1806 William Perigo visited Mary Bateman. His wife had suffered a minor heart attack and he was deeply concerned. Mary told him to bring one of his wife's petticoats which would be sent to Miss Blythe. Perigo willingly did so. Within a week Mary Bateman visited the Perigos at their Bramley home and told both husband and wife that she had received a letter from Miss Blythe to the effect that she was to sow four guinea notes contained in silken bags into the mattress of the couple's bed and in exchange for this she had to receive four guineas cash from them. With this done she advised the Perigos that Miss Blythe would contact them again in the very near future.

It was almost two weeks later when William Perigo received a letter from the alleged Miss Blythe. The letter explained that Perigo had to have two pieces of iron made into horseshoes and that these would then be affixed above the door of their home by Mary Bateman. Again a fee was charged and over the months which followed some £70 was extracted from the family via fraudulent claims.

In March 1807 the Perigos received the following letter: 'My dear friends, I will be obliged to you if you will let me have half a dozen of your china, three silver spoons, half a pound of tea, two pounds of loaf sugar, and a tea canister to put the tea in, or else it will not do – I durst not drink out of my own china. You must burn this with a candle.'

The articles requested were sent and the Perigos eagerly awaited further instructions. They had not long to wait for in April the following letter arrived at their home:

'My dear friends, I will be obliged to you if you buy me a camp bedstead, bed and bedding, a blanket, a pair of sheets, and a long bolster must come from your house. You need not buy the best feathers, common ones will do. I have laid on the floor for three nights, and I cannot lay on my bed owing to the planets being so bad concerning your wife, and I must have one of your buying or it will not do. You must bring down the china, the sugar, the caddy, the three silver spoons, and the tea at the same time when you buy the bed, and pack them up all together. My brother's boat will be up in a day or two, and I will order my brother's boatman to call for them at Mary Bateman's, and you must give Mary Bateman one shilling for the boatman, and I will place it to your account. Your wife must burn this as soon as it is read or it will not do.'

The Perigos spent sixteen guineas in purchasing the aforesaid articles and had them deposited at the Lion and Lamb Inn, Kirkgate, Leeds to be collected by the boatman. The letters began to arrive with more frequency and at the end of April a further letter arrived, the consequences of which were of a more serious nature:

'My dear friends, I am sorry to tell you you will take an illness in the month of May next, one or both of you, but I think both, but the works of God must have its course. You will escape the chambers of the grave; though you

seem to be dead, yet you will live. Your wife must take half a pound of honey down from Bramley to Mary Bateman's at Leeds, and it must remain there till you go down yourself, and she will put in such like stuff as I have sent from Scarbro' to her, and she will put it in when you come down, and see her yourself, or it will not do. You must eat pudding for six days, and you must put in such like stuff as I have sent to Mary Bateman from Scarbro', and she will give it to your wife, but you must not begin to eat this pudding while I let you know. If ever you find yourself sickly at any time, you must take each of you a teaspoonful of this honey; I will remit twenty pounds to you on the 20th day of May, and it will pay a little of what you owe. You must bring this down to Mary Bateman's and burn it at her house, when you come down next time.'
Mary Bateman supplied the Perigos with a white powder and advised them to use it according to instruction, otherwise they would be killed. A further letter received on May 5th instructed them to administer the powder to puddings which they should eat every day for six days, they were further told that should they fall ill during this time then no medical advice should be sought. The couple managed to stomach the puddings for five days. However, on the sixth and final day William Perigo found it impossible to swallow more than a couple of mouthfuls, whereas his wife ate four or five spoonfuls. Almost instantly the couple were overcome with severe stomach pains with Mrs Perigo suffering the worst of these. Yet she refused to allow her husband to call for medical assistance. With the puddings consumed the Perigos returned to eating the honey supplied by Mary Bateman. Religiously Mrs Perigo swallowed mouthfuls of the stuff on a daily basis, whereupon her condition deteriorated until she died on the 24th May.

The local surgeon, Mr Chorley, was called to the house and ascertained that Mrs Perigo had died by virtue of being poisoned, a fact which was confirmed by the sudden death of the family cat after it too had eaten some of the honey and pudding. Strangely no action was taken to definitely confirm the cause of death and the matter seemed to have been forgotten. William Perigo contacted Mary Bateman and told her of his wife's death – there seemed no suspicion by the man that his wife may have deliberately been poisoned. Perigo received various further letters from Miss Blythe instructing him that his wife had not obeyed the directions she gave, hence her death. Perigo maintained his total belief in Miss Blythe and Mary Bateman.

But William Perigo did become a little concerned by the lack of attention he was now receiving from Miss Blythe and Mary Bateman. He decided he had suffered enough and took the decision to tear open the mattress of his bed and retrieve the four guinea notes and pieces of gold which had been placed there during his wife's illness. With the best intentions Perigo tore open the four silk purses and his heart sank with the realisation of what had actually occurred. Instead of the anticipated money he found rotten cabbage leaves and old farthings! At once he notified the authorities and Mary Bateman was arrested on suspicion of murder.

The authorities carried out a thorough search of her home and found much of the property which was allegedly sent to Miss Blythe in Scarborough and a bottle containing arsenic was found in her pocket; the evidence was there for all to see!

On Friday 17th March 1809 Mary Bateman was brought to trial at York Castle before Sir Simon Le Blanc. It was quickly proved that neither Miss Blythe nor Mrs Moore existed. Bateman had sent letters to the Perigo family via Scarborough and had them re-directed. Mr Chorley the surgeon told how he had found traces of arsenic in the remainder of the pudding and honey found in the Perigo house. William Driffield, the Constable who arrested Bateman, explained how he had found a square bottle containing arsenic on Mary Bateman at the time of her arrest. Bateman continued to deny everything which was alleged against her, but this gave her little credibility as the case against her grew in magnitude. Eventually the jury found her guilty of murder and she was duly sentenced to death. Upon hearing the sentence Mary turned to one of of her gaolers and informed him that she was pregnant. The gaoler at once approached the bench and discreetly whispered this information to the judge. At once the doors to the courtroom were closed allowing no one to exit. This was done because the judge now required twelve women to act as a 'Jury of Matrons' who were to examine the prisoner to ascertain if she spoke the truth in relation to her pregnancy. The actual law at that time dictated that the delinquent had to be over four and a half months pregnant, otherwise the death penalty would proceed. The 'Jury of Matrons' could find no evidence to dictate that Mary Bateman was beyond the required stage of pregnancy and so the death penalty stood.

During her confinement in the condemned cell Mary displayed a calm attitude and did not seem too concerned as to her circumstances. The day prior to her execution she wrote to her husband enclosing her wedding ring, requesting that he pass it on to their daughter. The letter contained a confession of guilt relating to the many frauds but a denial as to willingly causing Mrs Perigo's death. This denial continued right up to her execution on 20th March 1809. After being allowed to hang for the requisite period, the body was cut down and removed to Leeds General Infirmary to be anatomised. Such was the enthusiasm shown by the public attempting to view the body that there was little alternative but for the hospital to put the body on view. Astutely they charged some two and a half thousand persons threepence and raised over £30. Later, her skin was tanned and distributed to anyone who applied for a portion.

It was never confirmed just how many gullible people were caught within the sinister web woven by the wicked witch of the North, but one thing which seems certain is the fact that even today we still have similar confidence tricksters amongst us. Thankfully as a nation we are a little less gullible than Mary Bateman's clients.

ALL LOST FOR LOVE

SITUATED close to the western boundaries of West
Yorkshire, Todmorden is a busy industrial place and
has in the past had the curious anomaly of being claimed
by both counties of Yorkshire and Lancashire. There are
those who still refer to it as 'Honest John's Town', a
reference to John Fielden MP, who was a local man who
dedicated most of his time to fighting for the rights of factory
workers. The novelist, William Holt, whose many novels
often depicted the countryside of this district, once lived in
an old Elizabethan house in the town. In mid Victorian times
the community was slightly more secluded and thus self
reliant. During this era most people would know much
about their neighbour, and such was the case in 1867 when
the 36 year old Reverend Anthony John Plow gave advice to
one of his servants about her relationship with a local man.

The Reverend Plow had been vicar of Todmorden for
some three years, taking up home in the vicarage close to the
church, during which time he acquired an unenviable
reputation for employing servant girls who tended to leave
the community in typical Victorian disgrace: pregnant. The
Reverend decided that enough was enough and that he
would closely monitor all future relationships and forbid any
clandestine assignations at the vicarage. Sadly another such
relationship had evolved, that between 17 year old Sarah
Elizabeth Bell, a cook at the Plow household, and a 23 year
old weaver by the name of Miles Weatherill. Miles worked
for Messrs Lord Brothers in the town and lived in Back
Brook Street with his widowed mother and sister. He
displayed academic qualities which had been nurtured at

York Street Sunday School, then more lately at Christ Church over which the Reverend Plow had charge. The vicar was aware of the weaver's deep and morose character. He seemed to attach himself passionately to whoever would show him attention. There had been many altercations between the Reverend and Weatherill during the summer months of 1867 for his moods were upsetting to many of the parishioners and to Plow himself. It therefore came as some surprise to Plow when he heard that Weatherill had been visiting his servant Sarah Bell at the vicarage during his periods of absence. Initially the Reverend attempted to discourage young Sarah from seeing Weatherill, explaining the trouble she could find herself in while courting a person who seemed destined for trouble. However, the young girl did not appear to take any notice of the Reverend's interference and continued to meet her paramour.

The situation seemed to deteriorate leaving Plow with no other option but to confront Weatherill. The latter was left in no doubt that if he continued to see Sarah Bell then she would be dismissed from the service of the household and returned to her home in York. Weatherill was furious and explained that the relationship was born of love not lust, but Plow was in no mood for such sentimental statements and told Weatherill to terminate the relationship at once. Despite such warnings the relationship continued, causing great consternation amongst the household staff at the vicarage. During this time there was a conflict of loyalties, other members of staff being no longer prepared to tell untruths about the continued relationship. Loyalty was in the end to the master of the house and not an impetuous child. Matters came to a head when Jane Smith, a nurse at the vicarage, caught the courting couple together and overheard them discussing their defiance towards the Reverend. The young nurse hurried back to the vicarage and at once informed the Reverend what she had seen and heard.

So on the 31st day of October 1867, Sarah Elizabeth Bell was dismissed from her position and returned to her home in York. From the conversation held between the Reverend and Sarah Bell the latter quickly realised that someone had informed Plow of certain facts and the only person who she could identify as so treacherous was the nurse Jane Smith!

Sarah Bell travelled to her home on the 1st November accompanied by Miles Weatherill who stayed with the Bell family for a number of days before returning to Todmorden. He had made the decision to leave Christ Church Sunday School because of the obvious animosity present between himself and Plow. Further to this, Plow had denied him several opportunities of becoming a Sunday School teacher, a point which Weatherill firmly held against him.

Miles sent numerous letters to Sarah, reiterating his love for her and how he wished she would return to Todmorden and be with him forever. However, Sarah was not so enthusiastic and she replied to the letters in a cool but sensible manner, trying not to hurt Weatherill too much, but making it quite clear that she was not going to return to Todmorden. Perhaps her parents had denied such an option. Certainly they must have felt that Weatherill was the root of their daughter's dismissal from an excellent position.

Weatherill and Plow had various arguments over the

Murderer Miles Weatherill and his victim Reverend Plow.

following weeks, all based around the Reverend's dismissal of Bell. Plow was unmoved by such actions and attempted to comfort Weatherill, explaining that he should get on with his life as Sarah Bell had now found alternative employment in York and would not have the opportunity to return to his arms. Such words only infuriated Weatherill, who already knew of his lover's new employment and hardly needed Plow to rub salt into his wounds. Refusing to allow their relationship to end, Weatherill set off for York on Saturday 28th February 1868 to see Sarah.

It appears that he finally accepted the fact that the relationship was finished though before he left Sarah on Monday 2nd March he argued with her about keeping the letters she had sent him in the past. But the pressures of such a long distance love affair were exaggerated by Weatherill's frame of mind, giving rise to thoughts of revenge upon the vicar's household, especially Jane Smith, whom he now blamed for losing the love of his life.

On returning to Todmorden later that evening, Miles Weatherill met with some friends who he remained with until approximately 10.00 pm. None of those present noticed anything different about him but upon leaving the group he went to the Black Swan Public House where he drank a glass of whisky before leaving and making his way to the Christ Church vicarage.

The vicarage was by virtue of its position secluded from other houses in the immediate vicinity and the rear of the house provided unhindered access. Weatherill went directly to the rear kitchen door. It was around 10.30 pm and the Plow household were in the initial stages of retiring to bed. Opening the unlocked door he was now within the kitchen and using a piece of string he attempted to tie the kitchen door knob to the inner passage door knob, thus making them secure should anyone attempt to open them from outside. During this act a servant attempted to gain entry into the kitchen but found it secured. Whoever was within was creating much noise and seemed to be in distress. The

servants, Elizabeth Spink and Mary Hodgeson ran for
Reverend Plow and told him of the commotion.

The reverend left the house via the front door and went
round to the rear where Weatherill was now lying in wait.
He at once lunged at Plow and during the ensuing struggle
Weatherill attempted to shoot Plow. However, the pistol
failed to go off. Then the demented lover produced a hatchet
which had been tucked inside his specially adapted leather
waistband. The hatchet crashed down upon the Reverend's
head. Amazingly Plow was able to snatch another pistol
from Weatherill thus momentarily forcing his attacker back.
Both men were soon wrestling and in the struggle broke into
the passage and into the full view of the now hysterical
housemaids. Somehow Plow broke free and ran for his life
to the home of William Greenwood, a local auctioneer and
near neighbour.

Meanwhile back inside the vicarage Miles Weatherill
caught sight of Jane Smith and at once rushed at her with the
hatchet raised high above his head. Within a split second it
was crashing through the defenceless girl's skull. The
momentum allowed her to get to the drawing room where
she was quickly followed by Weatherill who then shot her
twice through the head. Turning his attention to a figure
standing on the first floor landing, Weatherill seemed
hypnotised as he climbed the stairs screaming out 'Sarah –
Sarah'. The figure at the top of the stairs was nursemaid to
Mrs Harriet Louisa Plow, who had given birth to a daughter
just three weeks earlier. The maid attempted to bar entry
into her mistress's room, but Weatherill overpowered her
and entered Harriet Plow's room. Producing yet another
pistol from his armoury belt he fired it at Mrs Plow who lay
upon the bed. The shot misfired and so Weatherill used a
poker which he had found in the kitchen and smashed it
down upon Mrs Plow's face. The weight and force of the
three foot long object broke her nose. By this time some of
the servants had also fled the house in search of assistance.
This was already on its way as neighbour William

Greenwood had sought the help of a few other local men.

A number of men arrived at the house anticipating a violent struggle, yet upon their arrival they found Miles Weatherill somewhat subdued. He gave himself up to George Stansfield (the clerk of the church) without any further struggle and while awaiting the arrival of the local police constable he actually held a conversation with his captors, in particular with Mr Gleddill, his former school teacher. Weatherill said to him that it must have come as some surprise that one of his best scholars should end up in such dire circumstances. Police Constable Taylor soon arrived and arrested Weatherill who was then taken to and secured in the lock up at Toadcarr. It was later confirmed that Weatherill had taken an armoury of weapons with him to the vicarage including four loaded pistols, one hatchet, 27 bullets, 4 oz of shot, a number of caps and a small powder flask. The loaded pistols were found to contain two bullets in each and were loaded to within an inch of the muzzle. Also found upon Weatherill was a prayer book, a watch and a letter bearing the postmark 30th October which was seemingly sent from the vicarage to him. It read:

My Dear Miles,

Please do not come any more because there has been such a row. My dear Miles, I am very sorry to disappoint you but mother says it cannot be now for one thing. You must guess the rest, as I have to do, but I can tell you it is quite a great disappointment to me as it would be to you. If it is convenient for you to be at the station on Friday morning, at seven o'clock, I should so much like to see you again. It is hard to part with you, my dear own boy, but you must not fret, for I shall have you as well away as here. You know it is hard-hearted long parted, so I must say goodnight my dear, for it is bedtime, with a kiss I remain, yours ever.

Sarah. E. Bell.

During his detention in the lock up, Miles seemed quite cool, calm and collected about the whole affair, but he failed to take much sleep. At around 2.00 am he ate food then followed this at 6.00 am with a hearty breakfast. Throughout this time he continually discussed his dastardly work with his guardians and informed them that he was annoyed that he had not also killed Mr and Mrs Plow.

At 5.30 pm on Tuesday 3rd March Weatherill was brought before a special hearing consisting of Mr A Ormenrod, Mr John Fielden and Mr Joshua Fielden. Mr Gould appeared for the prosecution and informed the authorities that Mr and Mrs Plow were unable to attend through the injuries sustained and shock symptoms. Five charges were brought against the prisoner: the murder of Jane Smith; attempting to shoot Reverend Anthony John Plow with intent to murder him; with feloniously wounding the Reverend AJ Plow with a hatchet with intent to murder him; with shooting Harriet Louisa Plow, with intent to murder her; with feloniously wounding her with a poker, with intent to murder her.

The official inquest commenced Wednesday 4th March, at the Swan Inn. Dr Cockcroft, the physician who had performed the post mortem described the injuries found upon the remains of Jane Smith; there were several cuts to the head and neck, the right hand was almost severed in her attempts to defend herself from the hatchet blows raining down upon her and two bullets were found in her brain causing instantaneous death. The Reverend Plow (also examined by the doctor) had suffered two fearsome scalp wounds and a deep vertical wound in the temporal region. There was a great deal of blood lost during the attack, yet the Reverend insisted upon giving evidence at the inquest, probably much against his doctor's wishes.

During the inquest Plow was cross examined by Weatherill and was asked why he had refused permission for him to see Sarah Bell. He sincerely replied that she (Sarah) was too young for such a relationship. The questioning went to and fro and was based around this one point with the Reverend visibly annoying Weatherill with his direct response.

Weatherill was accused of the murder of Jane Smith and committed for trial at the Manchester Assizes. He made a somewhat dramatic plea that he now hoped that Mr and Mrs Plow and God would forgive him for his sins. He added that had he been given the privilege which he requested from Mr Plow (Sunday School teaching post) then he would never have found himself in this predicament. The Plow family must have felt quite relieved that the case against Weatherill was not to be a protracted affair causing them further stress and grief. Sadly the grief already forced upon the household was about to worsen, for on Thursday 12th March the month old daughter of the Plows suddenly died. This appeared to destroy the Reverend Plow's will to survive his horrific injuries, and he too died a few hours after his infant daughter. The official cause of his death was the result of blood loss and damage to the brain. Father and daughter were buried together in Christ Church, in a location which was near to the grave of Jane Smith, the funeral being attended by almost the whole town.

The final resting place of Reverend Plow and his daughter Hilda in Todmorden parish church graveyard.

Miles Weatherill was finally brought to trial on Friday 20th March with Mr Justice Lush presiding. The prosecution was represented by Mr Campbell-Foster while the defence offered Mr Torr. The trial was a straightforward affair. Weatherill pleaded not guilty to murder but this was easily disproved. The defence offered insanity as a plea but nobody was fooled by this and the jury found him guilty within just three minutes! The one sensation of the trial was when Sarah Bell took to the stand, her face covered by a black veil. During the questioning she admitted to leading Weatherill to believe that it was Jane Smith who had told tales to the Plows, yet it transpired that she had also confessed the assignations herself so perhaps falsely accused Jane Smith! At no point during her time in the witness box did Bell glance towards her ex-paramour, a point which seems to have greatly upset the various and many members of the press who were present!

Miles Weatherill was sentenced to death by hanging at 8.00 am Saturday 4th April 1868. During the interim period he wrote a number of letters to friends and family, on the whole displaying much remorse for his actions. On Thursday 2nd April Sarah Bell visited him in the condemned cell of New Bayley Prison, Salford, together with his mother. The meeting was, as can be expected, an emotional one, Sarah found it difficult to contain her emotions and sobbed inconsolably throughout the encounter, which was soon over.

At 8.00 am Saturday 4th April 1868 Weatherill took his last steps upon this earth to the public gallows erected outside the prison. He was executed along with another murderer and the crowds who were in their thousands screamed ecstatically as both men died at the hands of the executioner, William Calcraft, who later confirmed that the last words which Miles Weatherill murmured were 'God have mercy upon my soul'.

The crime cases of so many killers are filled with 'ifs and buts' yet this case seems to have hinged upon the attitude

Todmorden parish church with the vicarage next to it on the left.

displayed by an upright man of principle towards the reputation of his household and its staff. Did he really care about whether or not Sarah Bell would be hurt by her relationship with Weatherill or was he more concerned about the possible scandal caused by another member of his staff succumbing to the delights of a sexual encounter? We will never know.

A DEVOTED HUSBAND?

A GENTLEMAN of considerable wealth, with no obvious acquaintances which one could suspect as being anything other than platonic, displays sincere devotion towards his most treasured possession, his wife. He has nothing to gain from his wife's death, either financially or materially and there is nothing to suggest that the couple have anything but a close and permanent relationship. In 1855 one such man was charged with murder, no ordinary murder mind you, but the murder of his wife by poison. Could a devoted husband actually commit such a heinous act? The circumstances surrounding the case are shrouded in mystery, certainly, to this day many local people still argue the point as to who was guilty or innocent in Victorian Yorkshire's most northerly outpost.

Great Burdon is situated to the east of Darlington, and in 1855 it was part of the North Riding. Typical of many such communities, the people of Great Burdon were a concerned and inquisitive lot and not much which transpired within their village went unnoticed. However, when Doctor Jackson of Darlington called round to see Jane Wooler at her home not many eyebrows were raised. Jane Wooler was the daughter of a surgeon and was married to Joseph Snaith Wooler, a respectable and fairly affluent character. Jane Wooler had relatives within the community and this may have been the obvious reason why the couple had returned to live there after living for several years in India.

Jane Wooler was always susceptible to colds and illness. Her weak constitution was well known to Doctor Jackson and villagers alike. Her husband had summoned the doctor as Jane was suffering badly from stomach pains which he had apparently thought was indigestion. The Doctor explained that he felt that Jane was suffering from a severe bowel irritation and advised her to remain in bed for a few days, he then left. After his visit Jane's health did not seem to improve. Indeed she suffered frequent and horrendous bouts of vomiting which caused her husband more concern as it seemed obvious to him that the perceptions of Doctor Jackson were far from correct. With this in mind he called another doctor for a second opinion. Doctor Davy was suspicious of a number of things relating to the illness and he called in a colleague named Doctor Hazlewood who had a more specialised practice. Hazlewood realised that nefarious activities were afoot and decided to put Jane on a closely monitored diet. This he felt would prevent the cause of the vomiting, either through consuming drugs, or certain foods or fluids. The medications prescribed by him had to be injected and Joseph Wooler was shown how to administer these. Unfortunately Doctor Hazlewood's assistance came too late to save Jane Wooler's life and she died on the 27th June 1855. She lay for just two days before being buried on the evening of 29th June. The speed of the funeral caused much speculation among the community, fuelled by Doctor Jackson's refusal to sign the death certificate as he was concerned about the cause of death.

An inquest into Jane Wooler's death took place on the 14th of July 1855. As though to deter the rumours, Joseph Wooler explained to the coroner that he had no insurance on his wife's life, nor had he any profit to gain from her death. A basket of bottles containing various poisons was discussed and Wooler explained that this was a souvenir from India which was held within his home under strict security measures. The coroner had no option but to authorise the exhumation of Jane Wooler's remains. This action was vindicated by the verdict: that Jane Wooler died of poisons administered by a person or persons unknown.

There was discontent at this verdict amongst those who

realised that Jane Wooler had not died by natural causes. Her family were furious and laid the blame firmly at Joseph Wooler's door. Jane's brother went to the magistrates and laid information relating to the fact that two of the three doctors who had tended to his sister were of the opinion that she had been murdered by her husband, who had a reasonable knowledge of the scientific uses of poisons and cognate subjects. A warrant for Joseph Wooler's arrest was issued and he was duly detained. During a subsequent search of his house on the 28th July of the same year by Inspector Robinson of the North Riding Police, two baskets of bottles and two syringes were seized. The Inspector had no idea what the bottles contained but was well aware of their possible contents and their vital value as evidence.

Joseph Wooler was brought before the local Police court on the 30th July. Doctor Jackson gave evidence as to his personal suspicions pertaining to the use of poison in this case and that he believed it to be arsenic. He further related that during one visit to the house Joseph Wooler had shown him a basket containing numerous bottles of poisons including strychnine, iodine tincture and a bottle of Fowler's arsenic. The basket was produced in the court. However the doctor could not find the Fowler's arsenic, nor could it be found within the Wooler house. Jackson explained that during the deceased's final few days he had obtained a specimen of urine from her. This he sent to a Doctor Christison in Edinburgh, in order that it could be analysed and the results of this analysis concluded that the urine contained traces of arsenic.

Doctor Hazlewood told how he too suspected foul play during his treatment of the deceased. He had spoken with Jackson and both men were of the opinion that Joseph Wooler was in fact poisoning his wife. This was pure supposition as despite their suspicions, neither doctor could provide vital evidence which conclusively proved that Wooler had murdered his wife. Other witnesses were called. A housemaid explained that during her employment at the household she had not witnessed any sign of malice or ill treatment of her mistress by Joseph Wooler. Indeed, during her illness he had been greatly concerned as to her physical state. The two baskets containing the various bottles of poisons were identified as having been seen within the Wooler house. A further witness explained how shortly after Jane's death he had expected to find Joseph Wooler in a deep state of mourning but instead he had displayed absolute callousness and a cold attitude.

A surgeon named Fothergill gave damning evidence which would surely condemn Wooler to an early grave. Apparently Wooler had visited the surgeon and had discussed his wife's physical problems, explaining that he was administering nutritious injections but his apparatus was faulty and continually failed to work. He requested to borrow the surgeon's enema syringe. Fothergill permitted him to do so and the said item was returned just a few days later when it was locked away without further thought. When he had learned of Jane Wooler's death he recalled loaning the syringe and had checked it over. Within it he had found traces of arsenic. It seemed more than probable that Wooler had been feeding his wife poison anally rather than orally! The next major witness called was Doctor Alfred Taylor, an eminent pathologist of the time who had examined the exhumed remains. Again the evidence was critical. Taylor had found traces of arsenic in the rectum, heart and lungs of Jane Wooler. More telling was the fact that the majority of the arsenic had been found in the rectum!

Despite his pleas of innocence, Joseph Wooler was committed for trial for murder at the Durham Assizes. The trial commenced on the 7th of December 1855 before Mr Baron Martin. Wooler pleaded not guilty and once again the evidence heard at the Police Court was repeated and one should imagine it would have been sufficient to convict Joseph Wooler of murder. However, the defence counsel led by Mr Sergeant Wilkins queried every piece of so called evidence. They cast aspersions upon the medical practitioners and surgeons and provided some excellent character references for Joseph Wooler. To be quite frank, they clouded issues, causing confusion and thus detracted from the direct evidence. The prosecution led by Mr Edward James QC had been supremely confident that the evidence they provided would be sufficient. Perhaps they were arrogant but most certainly they failed to force home crucial points of evidence. One such point undoubtedly swayed the opinions of the judge and jury alike. Mr Sergeant Wilkins questioned the professionalism of the three doctors who had treated Jane Wooler. Each of the doctors had told the court that they were united in their opinion that whilst treating Jane they believed her husband to have been poisoning her. A serious accusation, yet not one of them informed the correct authorities of their suspicions. Instead they continued to treat Jane Wooler in the full knowledge that more poison would be administered! The prosecution could provide no answer for such blatant failures. The inference was that the doctors had increased the chances of their patient's death. The jury retired for just ten minutes before returning with a verdit of 'Not Guilty' against Wooler!

And so the case of Jane Wooler went unsolved. Had her husband indeed administered the poisons or were there other parties involved? The case was so straightforward and the verdict was undoubtedly incorrect. Why was Joseph Wooler allowed to walk free? True, the lacklustre attitude of the prosecution counsel failed to prove the case but there were those who believed some other influence was present within the court. Joseph Wooler was believed to have made various comments during the trial which had been attributed to the Society of Freemasons. Is it possible that the judge, being a fellow 'mason', influenced the jury to their final verdict? We shall never know, for all the players in this Victorian drama are now dead and Joseph Wooler took his grim secret to the grave with him.

THAT WILL DO FOR HIM!

AFTER its foundation on the 1st January 1848 the Bradford Borough Police made its headquarters at 24-26 Swaine Street. The premises also housed fire appliances as the police held a dual responsibility as fire fighters. The new surroundings and new style of policing were enthusiastically received by Bradford's public who anticipated increased security. The new police settled into the community quite nicely and facilities improved by the year with new fangled ideas being put into practice as economic policing was introduced.

By 1876 the force was superficially efficient though many problems were to arise for its officers. John Henry Johnson was to be one such problem. Johnson had emigrated to America in 1868 with his wife where they opened a small general dealers business. The couple struggled and in May 1876 Johnson returned to Bradford leaving his wife and son in America with the promise (empty, as it transpired) that their fares back to England would be forwarded forthwith.

Johnson was not a particularly honest individual. He frequented the kind of bars where he could associate with villains and whores. Being alone in Bradford Johnson lived the life of a single man and he soon met with a local woman of bad repute by the name of Amelia (Ann) Sewell. It was not too long before the couple were living together in Moss Street, Bradford.

Boxing Day 1876 saw Johnson and Sewell dress in their best clothing, partake in a spot of lunch, and leave their home for the Britannia Inn in the Wakefield Road area of the town. The drinking session lasted for most of the afternoon and the couple were joined at various intervals by friends and acquaintances of Sewell, including Amos Waite who was apparently very well known to her. Early in the evening the couple crossed the road and visited the Bedford Arms. Whilst there Amelia Sewell again bumped into Amos Waite who, with a stomach full of ale, decided to make amorous advances to her. She shouted out for Johnson to come at once which he did and a small scuffle ensued, resulting in Johnson biting Waite's finger and drawing blood. The scuffle was broken up by landlord Tommy Morgan and the men thrown out. Normally such a situation would have ended there and then, but Johnson was a man who bore grudges and he did not like the way Waite had been familiar with his woman. He decided to seek his revenge.

Johnson returned to his Moss Street home, collected his small Colt revolver and returned to the Wakefield Road area with Amelia Sewell by his side. It was not too long before he encountered Amos Waite who had just returned there, having bathed his wounded finger at home. Upon seeing Waite, Johnson exclaimed 'Now I will do for him' and simultaneously raised his arm and hand in which he held the loaded revolver. Amelia Sewell asked him not to fire but Johnson ignored her pleas and there was a sharp crack and a flash as the revolver was fired at the shocked Amos Waite. Johnson callously said 'That will do for him' as Waite collapsed to the ground clutching his left side and shouting 'Oh, I am done for!' He died almost immediately. Johnson turned on his heels and took off along Bedford Street but was followed by a witness to the murder, Benjamin Clarke, who summoned the assistance of a Mr Thomas Denby in wrestling Johnson to the ground and seizing the revolver, the prisoner was then marched to the Police station where he was detained.

Amos Waite was taken back to his home in Frederick Street. Doctor Lodge arrived and pronounced him dead from a bullet wound which had entered the left side of his chest above the nipple and entered the heart. Amos Waite left behind a grieving wife and six unfortunate children. Meanwhile back at the Police station Superintendent Laycock interviewed Johnson after the latter had recovered from the effects of drink and duly charged him with murder.

The case was brought before the Honourable Mr Justice Lopes at the Leeds Assizes on Monday 12th March 1877. Johnson pleaded not guilty to the charges made against him and so the trial commenced. Various witnesses told the court that Johnson and Waite both seemed to be suffering the effects of too much alcohol. The scuffle in the Bedford Arms was discussed as was the fact that Johnson had deliberately returned to his home in Moss Street to collect the revolver in order that he could use it to do harm to Waite. The case appeared straightforward until Doctor Samuel Lodge gave evidence. He explained that he had attended Waite's home and confirmed his death. Having done this he then visited the Police station where he saw Johnson asleep on a bench in a cell. He was discussing the matter with the duty Superintendent when a Constable came to tell him that Johnson was having some kind of fit. He had then comforted Johnson, who was indeed having some form of fit. The defence counsel asked if the fit was an epileptic one and the doctor confirmed this fact. The defence now had an opening which they wished to explore. 'One common form of insanity is the result of epilepsy is it not?' asked the defence, 'Yes, epilepsy is very often the forerunner to insanity' answered the doctor. The defence quickly followed this up with, 'I believe it is an admitted fact in your profession that insanity is frequently transmitted from a grandfather to a grandson, skipping one generation?' 'Yes' was the doctor's reply. It was then confirmed that Doctor Lodge had known Johnson's grandfather and had in fact treated him for epilepsy. It was added that the grandfather had died completely insane in the West Riding Asylum at Wakefield. The defence's ploy was to have Johnson found guilty but insane. But the ploy failed. The jury retired for just twenty five minutes before finding Johnson guilty of murder.

Donning the black cap Mr Justice Lopes addressed Johnson and said 'John Henry Johnson, you have been found guilty of the wilful murder of Amos Waite. I know not, I am sure, what it was that tempted you to do that wicked act, but it is impossible for anybody who has heard the evidence in this case to doubt that much of it is attributable to the effects of drink, that terrible vice which produces so much misery in this country.' After being sentenced to death Johnson was taken to Armley jail where he accepted his fate with great dignity. He wrote to Waite's widow and begged for her forgiveness, which he received on the eve of his execution.

The following morning at 6.30 am Johnson took communion and ate a large breakfast. At 7.45 am he was pinioned and taken to the gallows by his executioner, Mr Thomas Askern, the official hangman of Armley. Upon the gallows the noose was placed around Johnson's neck and the hood dropped over his head, Askern pulled the lever and with a crash the trap door opened to cast Johnson into oblivion. But suddenly there was a second crack and Johnson

Armley Prison in Leeds fills the skyline. John Henry Johnson was executed here, as was Charles Peace.

fell to the floor! The rope had snapped just above the noose; it had not been strong enough to support Johnson's weight! Panic ensued during which Johnson was untied and sat upon a chair. He was thus forced to watch his executioners prepare the gallows again for him. Johnson's feelings and mind at this time must have been filled with absolute horror. A second rope was fastened to the gallows and ten minutes later Johnson was again dropped through the trap door. This time he fell only a few feet and was seen to struggle and dance his way to death for several minutes before he finally went limp. It was later confirmed that Johnson had died as a result of the effects of asphyxia. Thomas Askern was never again to officiate at an execution at Armley!

A SUSPICIOUS CASE
IN SHEFFIELD!

SHEFFIELD in the Victorian era was similar to many other large towns, brimming over with highly industrious men who were forced to work long hours in order to earn a paltry weekly wage upon which they were often expected to maintain a family. Many thousands of women too were forced to earn their living by carrying out tasks in factories or any source of employment which would take them on. Sheffield, of course is perhaps synonymous with the steel industry and to this day Sheffield steel is claimed to be of a vastly superior class to its counterparts.

On Thursday 8th December 1881 a murder case was reported upon in the pages of the local press. Hardly sensational at that time, the report was deemed to warrant but a small paragraph in the summary of news section. It read:

'A suspicious case is being investigated by the Sheffield Police. Mr Thomas Skinner, a gentleman of independent means, living in Glover Road, Sheffield, became suddenly ill on Tuesday after taking dinner with his housekeeper. The latter also was affected with the same symptoms – those of poisoning – but subsequently somewhat recovered. Mr Skinner, however, succumbed. Kate Dover, the housekeeper, was taken home, and is in a critical state. Mr Skinner before dying declared that he had been poisoned. The fowl eaten at dinner was bought from a poulterer, who, at the housekeeper's request, removed the neck and inside. The poulterer says he and his family ate these parts for dinner themselves and sustained no ill effects, so that the fowl could scarcely have been the cause of death.'

Thomas Skinner was a local celebrity and artist of some notoriety (or etcher as he was titled by Victorian society). Fifty years old and a bachelor, he resided at number 24 Glover Road in the Sheffield district of Heeley along with his ex model Jane Jones and her husband. After the marriage Jane had remained at Skinner's home in the role of housekeeper which was a satisfactory arrangement for all, as it provided the Joneses with cheap accommodation, and much needed company for Skinner. The relationship between the trio was obviously quite good as Thomas Skinner actually included the Joneses in his will, with Jane being the principal benefactor. Undoubtedly there would be much financial stability from such a legacy as Skinner was known to be in a healthy financial state.

Things were to alter dramatically in the spring of 1880. Skinner had become acquainted with a pretty 25 year old confectioner Kate Dover who kept a shop in the London Road area of Heeley. It seems that Skinner had become obsessed by the young woman and had at once asked her if she would kindly sit for him for a portrait. Kate Dover pondered over the matter but eventually agreed to the request. It was an acquaintance which would eventually lead to Skinner's death!

The relationship between Dover and Skinner became deeper as the young woman began to call at Skinner's home in Glover Road with some frequency and it caused some concern to Skinner's immediate friends who warned him as to the possible disastrous consequences of an intimate relationship with a woman half his age.

Kate Dover was aware of the contempt displayed by Skinner's friends and especially that of Jane Jones and her husband who had openly warned Skinner that they distrusted her. However, Skinner seemed oblivious to the fact that Kate Dover's friendship with him may have been false and only a disguise to justify subsidising her welfare from his wealth. In the autumn of that same year Jane Jones and her husband moved out of 24 Glover Road in dispute with their friend and landlord over his attitude since encountering Miss Dover. Initially Skinner was none too concerned over this matter as he had identified a new opportunity in his life. Quite simply he would ask Kate Dover to move in with him! Yet for reasons best known to herself Dover declined the invitation but agreed to visit on a daily basis and to act as his housekeeper.

The months which followed were full of trouble and deceit as Skinner noticed that some of his smaller household valuables were disappearing, culminating in a minor confrontation when his suit went missing. Kate denied all such allegations and offered to end the liaison, but Skinner backed down and pathetically begged her to stay on. Just what else occurred during those troubled months we shall never be certain but one thing that can be confirmed is the fact that there was a dramatic change to Thomas Skinner's personality and emotions towards Kate Dover. She often told neighbours how he would hit and verbally abuse her; a fact which seems to have been substantiated by others who claimed to have witnessed such assaults.

The relationship between the artist and his housekeeper may be regarded as volatile and most certainly unpredictable, yet no one could have anticipated the emotional transformation which took place at 24 Glover Road in the months leading up to the summer of 1881. The couple were anything but discreet in showing their feelings for each other in public. Skinner was like a smitten youngster who had never been in love before – besotted is possibly the best manner in which to describe him. He discussed the possibility of altering his will in favour of Kate Dover and maintained his hope that she would one day be his bride. In reality Kate Dover was achieving her objective: to acquire as much of Skinner's wealth as she could. In order to secure her position and to possibly provide an alibi for herself, she told

Skinner and as many other friends of the artist as she could that Jane Jones had actually threatened to kill both of them before Christmas! Jane Jones heard of the malicious gossip being spread by Dover and was greatly angered by it. But being of a more stable and intelligent character she realised that it would be fruitless to confront Dover, as she would merely use it as more ammunition. Instead she sent Thomas Skinner a basket of vegetables as a gesture of her continuing friendship with the man. This totally undermined much of Kate Dover's immature actions in attempting to cause a rift between them!

By early December 1881 Kate Dover had decided upon a course of action which she felt appropriate in order to procure Skinner's wealth. On Sunday 4th December Thomas Skinner spent much of the day on his own and then, at around 6.30 pm he visited a local inn. He arranged to meet Kate at the establishment (The Big Tree Inn) later that evening. Prior to her arrival there she visited Hewitt's apothecary and purchased one ounce of arsenic. When asked why she required it Kate Dover explained that she was using it to colour dried flowers. She signed the poisons register and as she turned to leave the shop, Mr Hewitt, the shop owner, heard her mumble to herself on walking through the shop doorway, 'now I have it I shall take the lot.'

On Tuesday the 7th December Kate Dover sent housemaid Emma Bolsover to a shop in London Road, Heeley to purchase a chicken for the lunch that afternoon. While the maid was out Dover prepared the vegetables for the meal. These included some onions which had been sent with Jane Jones' gift to Skinner. Emma Bolsover returned with the chicken and saw Kate Dover peeling the onions. She made a spurious claim to feeling unwell because of a strange aroma emanating from the onions, but the maid could perceive no strange smell. Almost immediately she was sent out again, this time to purchase some gin and upon her return everything was prepared. Two separate lots of sage and onion stuffing seemed rather extravagant to the maid but she

The shop in London Road, Sheffield in the 1880s where Emma Bolsover purchased a chicken which was to be the death of Thomas Skinner.

did not dare query the reason for this. Kate Dover insisted upon not only preparing it but serving the meal as well. Thomas and Kate sat down and ate the chicken and trimmings prepared with Kate's own fair hands.

Having consumed much of what was on their plates Kate clutched her stomach and began to retch although she did not actually vomit. Thomas Skinner also complained of similar pains and vomited. His immediate suggestion was that Jane Jones had poisoned them both with the vegetables she sent. Kate sent for Doctor Harrison who on his arrival noted the serious condition of Thomas Skinner who was clearly suffering from the effects of poisoning. Both were given an emetic agent to induce vomiting and freely passed the meal which they had recently consumed. Thomas Skinner was in a more serious condition than Kate and was forced to retire to his bed, while Kate sat caringly by his side. At 8.30 that evening after many hours spent writhing in agony, the deep burning sensation within his stomach subsided as Thomas Skinner passed away. Doctor Harrison left 24 Glover Road taking with him samples of the last consumed meal and vomit from both Skinner and Dover.

The Police were informed and were requested to await the results of analysis upon the samples removed. Sure enough arsenic was found within Thomas Skinner's vomit and the stuffing prepared by Kate Dover. Curiously, no trace of arsenic was found in Kate Dover's vomit.

Inspector Bradbury of the Sheffield Police visited the scene and spoke with Emma Bolsover who informed him of all she knew and had heard from her sister who was a previous employee at the household. The case against Jane Jones was strengthened as most people spoke of her alleged threats to kill Skinner and Kate Dover. Then there was the question of the basket of vegetables sent to the house just five days prior to the tragic events. Enquiries were centred around Jane Jones who was interviewed by Bradbury. She denied ever uttering such threats. She further explained that her family had also eaten some of the vegetables she sent to Skinner, yet none of them had suffered any illness. The explanation supplied by Jane Jones was more than sufficient to satisfy the Inspector that she was innocent of any accusations made against her. The following day he again visited 24 Glover Road, on this occasion he spoke to Kate Dover. He was curious as to why she prepared two separate amounts of stuffing. When questioned, Kate implied that it was a mistake; she had made too much and so decided to cook the left over portion. He then asked if there was any poison in the house to which Kate pleaded ignorance of any knowledge of such a substance!

The Police Inspector was keen to catch the murderer and his suspicions were against Kate Dover. Visiting Hewitt's apothecary in London Road his Policeman's intuition paid dividends as Hewitt told him of Kate's recent visit and curious comments upon leaving the shop. The poison register clearly proved that she had indeed purchased one ounce of arsenic, so he returned to confront Dover with this new evidence. He was somewhat surprised to see Dover burning some papers in the drawing room fire. Kate told him that it was Thomas Skinner's last request that she should destroy some of his personal papers. Bradbury did not believe her and at once arrested her and she was conveyed to Armley Prison, Leeds, awaiting trial.

The case against Dover was convincing, yet just one thing plagued Inspector Bradbury and the prosecution – the lack of a motive! It was clear that she had played a role in his death but the severity of this could not be ascertained, nor was it ever to be. The defence counsel in the realisation that their client was guilty to some extent told the jury that Kate Dover had in fact placed arsenic in the stuffing mixture, but the dose was not anticipated as being lethal. She had expected it to cause him some discomfort and hoped to frighten Skinner into changing his will in her favour, the intent being to encourage his mistrust and hatred of Jane Jones!

Kate Dover was extremely unhappy about this situation and pleaded with counsel to present her with the opportunity of defending herself in the dock. It was, of course, too great a gamble for Mr Muir-Wilson to permit, most defendants actually talked themselves to the gallows when such requests were granted. Muir-Wilson denied her the opportunity and in his closing speech expounded upon Kate Dover's great respect for Thomas Skinner hence she would not have remained with him during his alleged bouts of violence. He created a superficial image of Dover while portraying her as genuine and caring! The ploy was successful as the jury after retiring for over two hours returned a verdict of guilty of manslaughter, and Dover was duly sentenced to penal servitude for the rest of her natural life.

The case aroused much consternation throughout Yorkshire. There was a common belief that Dover was guilty of murder and that her actions warranted nothing less than the death penalty. The pages of the local press dictated the local people's feelings towards the verdict. There was even a letter from one of the jurymen who claimed that he felt the verdict was an outrage against British justice.

The question of Kate Dover's premeditation and intention

still remains open to debate. Personally, I feel that she did escape justice. After all, the mere fact that she placed arsenic in Skinner's meal in the knowledge that small amounts were lethal is in itself a confession to reckless behaviour which should have been used against her. Furthermore, the analyst who examined the food prepared by her told the Police that there was sufficient arsenic within the food to kill in the region of two hundred or more people!

The final debate has to be regarding the contents of the papers which Dover was burning when visited by the Police Inspector. Had these contained Thomas Skinner's will in favour of her then it could have provided damning evidence against her. Similarly if the will had Jane Jones as the beneficiary then Dover would want it destroyed as she would lose everything. Granted that such conclusions are nothing more than assumptions, one must still ask oneself an extremely pertinent question; during the build up of animosity between Jane Jones and Kate Dover the question of who was named as beneficiary in Thomas Skinner's will was paramount. It was mentioned to friends and neighbours, and indeed, Skinner himself told Kate Dover that he would change it to her advantage. Yet despite a thorough Police search of 24 Glover Road, no last will and testament relating to Thomas Skinner was ever found! The reason has to be that Kate Dover destroyed it for one of the aforementioned reasons!

MURDER OF A
FISHER-LAD

A GUILTY conscience can cause certain individuals a great deal of grief. Others find it no problem to forget such guilt and it goes without saying that at some point in every person's life they have encountered such emotion. For most of us such emotions are of a trivial nature, yet there are many who have hidden guilt locked away in the darkest recesses of their minds; 'skeletons in their cupboards' as the popular phrase depicts. A number of individuals suffered greatly from such problems in the East Riding fishing port of Hull in 1882, for they had a guilt that not many others have to deal with, that of the knowledge of murder! Such individuals were sworn to secrecy, but found the burden too great to handle and so revealed one of the most barbaric stories to unfold in a British courtroom.

On Thursday 5th January 1882, Osmand Otto Brand, skipper and part owner of the Hull-based fishing smack *Rising Sun* entered the Parliament Street Police station in the port of Hull and spoke to Sergeant William Elliott. Brand told the duty officer that he wished to report the fact that one of his crew had fallen overboard at sea and subsequently drowned; the following is the entry made by Sergeant Elliott in the station occurrence book:

'Osmand Otto Brand, residing at Harrow house, Hessle Road, Hull and skipper and owner of the smack *Rising Sun,* reports that at about 5.30 am on the 1st of January 1882, they were trawling on the fishing ground about 120 miles from Spurn, when the cook, William Papper, 14 years of age, a native of Hull, was knocked overboard by the big foresail sheet and drowned. The smack was put about, and every effort was made to save him, but without avail. The body was not recovered.'

At that point in time there was little to suggest that Osmand Brand was anything but remorseful about the loss of the young fisher-lad and that he was stating anything but the truth. Brand knew the Papper family fairly well and had told the boy's father of the tragedy prior to reporting it to the authorities. William Papper had been apprenticed to Osmand Brand by his father Joseph Papper in the April of 1881; it was to have been a seven year apprenticeship. William had gone to sea on Thursday 17th December 1881. This was the last time his father had seen him alive. Apparently he was quite excited about the trip and was keen to please the skipper, Osmand Brand. Joseph Papper must have been himself quite thrilled to see the *Rising Sun* moored in the Albert Dock on Thursday the 5th of January 1882. He approached the ship and was met by Osmand Brand who bid him a good-day. He then added 'I've very bad news to tell you. Your little boy got knocked overboard by the big foresail on New Year's morning. I was down below, and they came and told me the boy was overboard. I ran up the ladder and let go the stopper to bring the ship round, but we could see nothing of him. He was called up at half past five in the morning, to get the breakfast ready, and they called him forward to help take the big foresail in.'

Accidents at sea were quite a common occurrence around seaports and the tragic loss was accepted by family and the authorities alike. After a brief investigation one or two ambiguities existed but nothing to cause too much concern, that is until the guilt ridden mind of one individual (who was part of the crew onboard the *Rising Sun*) caused him to visit the Police and make a remarkable statement which completely altered the complexion of the case. The statement of William John Dench read:

'I reside at No 18 Staniforth Place, Hessle Road, Hull, and

am second hand of the smack *Rising Sun,* owned by Osmand Otto Brand, who is also captain of the smack. About Thursday, 17th December last, I left Hull for the fishing ground in the *Rising Sun* as second hand, there being on board Mr Brand, the captain; Frederick Rycroft, the third hand; David Yates, deck chap; William Blackburn, apprentice; and William Papper, cook and apprentice. After the smack left the Albert dock she brought up at Sunk Island, and remained there all night. After we had cast anchor I was on deck with the captain and crew, when I heard the captain say to Papper 'Get me a lacing' (a lacing is used to tie the mainsail up). Papper went down into the cabin, and the captain followed him, as likewise Blackburn. I was standing on the deck at the companion ladder, which leads to the cabin, when I heard the captain say, 'Now you bugger, I'll pay you for telling lies about me. I have had something to do with your sister haven't I?' The boy commenced to cry, and said, 'I never said so.' He then commenced to thrash him, and as he did so, he said, 'Now you bugger, I have had something to do with your sister, and I'll do you.' I then went down into the cabin and found the captain beating Papper with a short piece of rope about one and half inches in thickness, with a knot at each end. He thrashed him for about five minutes. He struck him repeatedly on the head and face, and I saw the boy's nose bleeding, and his lips were swollen. The captain then told him to get washed, and called him a mucky bugger. The boy was crying, and appeared very much hurt from the beating he had received. Papper then at the captain's request, got the tea.

On Friday, the 23rd December, about nine o'clock in the morning, we were about 90 miles from Spurn Light. I was on the deck helping to mend the trawling line net, when I heard the captain say to Papper, 'Now this is all through you', referring to the damage the net had sustained through the warp having fouled, and I saw him strike Papper a blow with his clenched fist in the face, which knocked him down. He then ordered him to go forward, and stop there for three days, calling him a bugger at the same time. The lad at once got up. He was crying from the effects of the blow, and went forward. The captain followed him and said to him, 'Get up on that stay', pointing to it. Papper, who was still crying, did not get up, and the captain then said, 'You won't get up? Then I'll make you', and he then went up and got a bucket, which had a rope tied to it, and he dipped the bucket overboard and drew it up full of water, and threw it over him. He repeated this treatment five or six times. The lad then said, 'Don't throw any more water over me and I'll get up.' The captain then said harshly, 'Get on there', and I saw the lad mount the stay. He was wet through. The skipper then went to a small boat which was on deck, got a handspike and took it forward, and, handing the handspike to Papper, he said, 'Here take hold of this.' The lad Papper took the handspike, and did as he was told, holding on by one hand by the stay, and with the other hand he held the handspike with an end resting on the rail. The skipper then told us to go aft and get our dinners and we did so. Whilst we were having our dinners the skipper went back on deck, and I followed about ten minutes afterwards. I then saw the skipper in the act of thrashing Papper with a rope end. Papper at that time was on the deck forward, and had apparently got down from the place where we left him. I heard the skipper say to him, 'Get up on to the stay, you bugger.' Papper was crying, and did not get up, and I saw the skipper strike him several blows in the face with his clenched fist. Papper was lying on the deck, and the skipper was bending over him and striking him with his fist. The skipper next took hold of him by the back of his guernsey, and dragged him aft to a spot about six feet from the windlass, and Papper then got up onto his knees, and was about to go aft when the skipper dealt several blows with the end of a rope. The skipper then got the lantern halliards and tied them under

Papper's arms, and as he did so, he said, 'I'll hang you, you bastard.' The lad cried, 'Oh, don't hang me.' The skipper then put the end of the halliards round the winch, and called Blackburn to him. Blackburn then winched and turned the handle, Papper was drawn up about four feet from the deck. The skipper held on to Papper's legs to steady him, whilst being hauled up he screamed loudly, the crosstree holding the lantern halliards broke and Papper fell heavily onto the deck. Papper seemed to be insensible and was sent forward to the stem by the skipper.

The next morning (Saturday) about eight o'clock, before Christmas, I was on deck, and I saw the skipper and Papper forward. At the time I saw the skipper he was beating Papper with a rope's end. Papper was standing up on deck, and I saw the skipper leave off rope's ending him, and he struck him a heavy blow on the side of his head with his clenched fist, which knocked him down. I saw him jump onto Papper with both feet. He jumped onto his chest, and then knelt on him – on the chest, and reached for a rope, which was near and tied it round his neck and pulled both ends tight. It appeared to me that he was endeavouring to strangle him. I then rushed forward and took hold of the skipper by the shoulder and said, 'Leave off, or you will be killing the lad,' he said, 'I don't care, I'll kill the bugger.' He then got up off Papper and I stooped down and untied the rope from Papper's neck.'

The statement continued to depict the most horrendous torture imaginable towards any person, let alone a young boy. Passage after passage causes one to recoil in horror; god only knows what thoughts passed through William Papper's mind during the final hours of his life, though death must have been something of a relief compared to the living hell he had suffered on board the *Rising Sun*.

At 6.00 am on New Year's Day the lad finally died from his terrible treatment. William Dench's statement continued:

'He was dead. His eyes were black, and his countenance disfigured. The skipper said, 'What shall we do with him?'

I said, 'I don't know he is your apprentice.' He said, 'We shall have to throw him over board, he is too disfigured, we dare not take him back to Hull. You must keep Dave (meaning David Yates) on deck, and not let him see him, because I cannot trust him. He will spoil all. You are all in it as well as me.' The next morning at three o'clock, the skipper called me out and said, 'Give us a hand to get Papper on deck.' I got up and went to the bunk where the corpse was and assisted the skipper, Rycroft and Blackburn to carry it on deck again. The skipper then came down, and he got the deceased's clothes – trousers, shirt, and braces – and went on deck again. About half past five Rycroft came to the companion ladder and called out to me and the skipper, 'Jump out here, Papper is overboard."

An ignominious end to such a young life. Brand and Rycroft who were the main perpetrators of this wicked crime were arrested at once. Brand actually claimed that he was innocent and that each other member of the crew were as guilty if not more so than he. The East Riding Police took little notice of his malicious ramblings and he was tried at the Hull Assizes along with Frederick Rycroft. It is to be truly hoped they suffered in their final moments before expiring, their overwhelming guilt was and is clear to all who read or hear of the case. Perhaps one could point an accusing finger at William Dench, but his sense of duty caused by a guilt complex did allow him to relate the real truth behind the matter and ultimately bring two of Britain's most evil characters to justice.

Unfortunately for Dench many local people did not view his voluntary statement in the manner in which it was meant! A local press report of the day stated:

'The details of the alleged murder have created tremendous excitement amongst the fishing community of South Myton, and singularly enough the tide of popular indignation has set in against William John Dench, the man whose statements led to the apprehension of Brand, the skipper of the *Rising Sun*. Dench resides at 18, Staniforth Place, Hessle Road, and yesterday morning his house was beseiged by a large number of persons, who loudly declared their intentions of lynching him. Dench, with difficulty escaped, and the crowd was cleared away by the policeman who was on duty in that neighbourhood. The man was, however, followed by a dozen others, and it would have fared ill with him had he got into their hands. Fortunately for him he managed to keep clear of those who were on watch for him. Doubtless he will receive the protection of the police, as his evidence against Brand, the skipper, is of the gravest character.'

Sadly, the press like many of the fishing colleagues of Brand had forgotten the real tragedy of this affair, the murder of an innocent and defenceless young boy!

INDEX